YOGI ON DALAL STREET

ANCIENT WISDOM FOR MODERN DAY INVESTOR

ARUN THUKRAL

ISBN 979-8-89322-675-1

This book is dedicated to my wife Madhu and my daughter Anahita for their immense love and support throughout. Without them, this book would not have been possible.

Contents

About the Author

Arun Thukral is the professor of practice in Finance at KJ Somaiya Institute of Management in Mumbai. He is the former MD & CEO of Axis securities. He is a keen observer of yoga philosophy and uses various yogic concepts to explain investor psychology for effective wealth creation. He is also an angel investor and acts as a mentor for founders of startups in domains like FinTech, EdTech, HRTech etc. He is a distinguished and sought-after keynote speaker at leadership events. With his wealth of experience and expertise, he brings a unique perspective to the world of leadership, management and finance. In addition to his role as a keynote speaker, Mr. Arun Thukral also plays a vital role as an interviewer, engaging in insightful conversations with thought leaders who are CEOs of major finance companies. He is currently the acting chairperson of FPSB CFP Advisory Council India.

Arun contends that success in the market is closely tied to understanding investor psychology, and he actively seeks this connection by drawing on his avid interest in Yoga philosophy and incorporating its principles into investing. He is a certified Yoga practitioner from 'The Yoga Institute, Santa Cruz'. He uses different Yogic concepts to explain the investor psychology for effective implementation. He firmly believes the next decade belongs to the Indian retail investors. The Indian consumption story shall drive the retail investors towards sustained wealth creation. With India remaining the fastest growing economy in the world, the benefit of this growth is set to accrue to the equity holders more than anyone else. Thus, wealth creation shall be unparalleled in this asset class. He consistently advises his mentees to target equity as an investment focus, so as to grow their wealth over the long term and reap the benefits of a growing nation.

Acknowledgements

First and foremost, I would like to profoundly thank 'The Yoga Institute, Santacruz' for exposing me to the vastness that Yoga has to offer and for making me realize that there is more to it than asanas. I would specifically like to thank Smt. Hansaji, Director, The Yoga Institute. She has been a true inspiration and guiding force for me to explore different facets of Yoga. I also express my sincere thanks to senior sadhaks – Shri. Kartik and Shri. Niranjan for their unending guidance in the understanding of Yoga Sutra. Yoga has had a transformative effect on my life, particularly after I delved into Yoga philosophy, which served as the foundation for the inception of this book.

This book is the new edition of the original one published in 2018. I would like to extend my gratitude to Ms. Mansi Kwatra and Ms. Vyoma Shah for their relentless efforts in updating the original version of this book.

I would like to thank my former organisation, Axis Bank, especially Ms. Shikha Sharma, Mr. Rajiv Anand and Mr. Rajesh Dahiya for supporting and encouraging me to undertake this journey alongside my organisational responsibilities. To my colleagues Sandeep, Pankaj, Malini and Rohit for their ideas and for helping me shape this book. And last but not the least, a big thanks to Notion Press for believing in my vision and for sharing the conviction that this book can be of value to readers.

Foreword

By
Vallabh Bhanshali,
Meditator, Thought Leader, Investment Banker
and Co-founder of ENAM group

What you are about to read in the pages ahead is an amazing blend of Yoga philosophy and the art of creating phenomenal wealth through investing. The book outlines beautifully how our mind works and how we can take control of our mind, in order to arrive at the right investment ideas, or for that matter any useful ideas.

The book draws reference to the "Yoga Sutra", written thousands of years ago by Maharishi Patanjali. The Maharshi's Ashtanga Yog is an excellent compilation of all the Yogic traditions of his time (practices that unite the mundane with the Supreme) or one could say a great summary of Indian thought. It thus, is a commentary on the art of a very practical and systematic life. Until I came across his writing, I could have never imagined how well suited was the Yog philosophy for explaining the path to riches through value investing. But once it came to my hand, it seemed so very obvious! This is the genius of Arun Thukral. I attribute this genius to his deep desire to benefit his audiences from the wisdom of investing in the tremendous potential of this country, now that we seem to have given up defeatist policies for good. Never has investor psychology been explained with such clarity, using our ancient scriptures. When we read the utterances of Mr. Charlie Munger, the greatest repository of wisdom of our times, we come across copious references to the

European ancient scholars such as Cicero, Herodotus, etc. Here Arun brings us wisdom from much closer home and of levels unmatched anywhere in the world.

Just as the need for a healthy body to benefit from a healthy mind is obvious, so also, is the need to overcome lack of a certain amount of income and wealth to elevate one's life beyond the mundane struggle for well-being. That being said, making money grow faster is desired by most of us but hardly a few succeed. The stock markets behave in the same manner for everyone, so why is it that only a few succeed to earn a great fortune, while most go empty handed or with meager gains? The book reveals, the answer lies not in the market but within our own selves. We must train our minds first to see things with absolute clarity.

The reader gets two benefits for the price of one here, because his book besides the tips of investing also contains the key to unlocking the true potential of human life by drawing on the ancient secrets of Yoga Sutras.

Excellence in all aspects of life is more desirable than success, has been my goal and prescribed philosophy for all. We can control excellence but not success. The excellent are more likely to achieve sustainable success more than anyone else! Excellence in all spheres of life, be it mental, physical or financial. I fully concur with my dear friend and author of the book Arun Thukral, that one should not be apologetic about creating wealth. This book will benefit anyone who is interested in making their money grow. Anybody who can stay true to the principles outlined in this book and internalise the Yoga Mantras will surely accelerate the growth of their investments. I am sure the reader will be greatly inspired to make a deeper study of our Yog tradition and benefit way beyond wealth creation. I must re-emphasis what Arun does too, that investment is a great science and

art and one remains a student all one's life. Starting from this book, the layman must apply oneself to studying the field of investment in a constant and ever more thorough manner.

I wish Arun's desire to convert every reader into "The Yogic Investor" and a Yogi, by and by, succeeds handsomely.

– Vallabh Bhanshali

From the desk of
Smt. Hansa Jayadeva Yogendra,
Director, The Yoga Institute, Santacruz

Arun had joined 'The Yoga Institute' around five years back with an objective to attain physical well-being through Asanas. When he was introduced to Yoga philosophy, he realized the immense magnitude of Yoga and used it more as a way of life rather than only as the practice of Asanas. He incorporated this Yogic practice into his professional life as well and integrated various investment concepts with a number of Yoga principles. I am happy that he has penned down these thoughts and compiled this wonderful book. This book would provide a very different perspective to sound investing practices backed by powerful yoga sutras and would benefit anyone who is interested in growing both spiritual and material wealth. I wish Arun all the best in this endeavour.

From the desk of
Mr. Nilesh Shah,
Market Guru and
MD & CEO of Kotak Mutual Fund

Ancient Indian scriptures have been a rich source of knowledge. It has been a great endeavour by my dear friend Arun Thukral who by virtue of being head of a leading brokerage house has amalgamated his learnings about stock market investing with the age old yogic philosophy thus giving birth to the "Yogi on Dalal Street". His book is a masterpiece in itself, a sure shot guide for an investor, be it a fledgling one or a seasoned one. It helps one get rid of the misconceptions that have been developed among investors, cut teeth in the world of investments when equipped with the yogic knowledge. I would recommend each and every investor worth his salt to read this book and test it on every investment action enacted by him in past, present and that he is looking forward to undertake in future. Taking insights from my own journey in investing world, I find this book worthy enough to serve as a gospel for the investors.

From the desk of
Mr. Ramachandran Raman,
Director, KJ Somaiya Institute of Management

As someone from a non-finance background, I found Arun Thukral's book easy to read and follow. He presents complex ideas with simplicity and clarity. Arun seamlessly links principles of yoga and investing which is a very unique approach. In a way, he underscores the importance of health and wealth. Reading this book has been an enriching and enjoyable experience.

We have the privilege of having Arun as Professor of Practice at our Institute. His ability to translate theoretical knowledge into practical wisdom has been instrumental in shaping student's understanding of the financial landscape. The real-world applications and case studies he shares during his lectures have deepened their appreciation for the subject.

Introduction

अथ योगानुशासनम्

Atha Yoga-anushasanam

Now let us begin the discipline of Yoga

– 1.1 Patanjali Yoga Sutra

Puruṣhartha (पुरुषार्थ) is a composite Sanskrit word that combines the words purusha (पुरुष) and v artha (अर्थ). Purusha is a synonym for 'human' and artha means 'purpose' or 'object of desire'. Purushartha literally means the 'purpose of human existence' or 'object of human pursuit'. It is a key concept in Vedic philosophy that comprises four component pillars or pursuits. The four Puruṣharthas are Dharma (righteousness or moral values), Artha (prosperity or economic values), Kama (pleasure or love or psychological values) and Moksha (liberation or spiritual values).

There is an abundant corpus of literary material available on Dharma, Kama and Moksha in our ancient scriptures. Artha is least discussed and often underplayed, despite it being one of the four Purusharthas. This book has been written to give Artha its due position as a relevant human goal or pursuit. Typically, people do not associate Yoga with materialism or creating wealth. However, a closer look at ancient scriptures points out that Artha or economic values should be one of the key pursuits of human endeavour. It encourages Grihastas or householders to accumulate wealth unapologetically. There is nothing spiritual about being poor or in a state of deprivation. Some of the most elevated souls in the Indian tradition have been phenomenally rich.

In fact, this book began with my surprising albeit happy discovery that even the principles of Yoga point in the direction of wealth creation. Yoga vidya, contrary to popular belief, has way more to offer than the health benefits of asanas, which are but one limb or part of the system the ancients called eight-limbed-Yoga or 'Ashtang Yoga'. Yoga is a way of life. While most people relate Yoga mainly to Asanas (Yoga postures) or Pranayam (conscious awareness of breath), there is much more to Yoga than this. While Yoga Asanas and Pranayam help one attain a healthy body and a healthy mind, Yoga vidya helps one attain a much higher clarity of thought and enhances one's control on the mind. I was struck, in particular, by the profound philosophy of Yoga outlined in the Yoga Sutra written by Maharshi Patanjali almost two thousand five hundred years back and its universal application to almost all aspects of the modern world, as we know it today. As an investor, banker and former CEO of a firm that offers investment solutions, I saw the tremendous value that the Yoga Sutra could provide to investors at large. Life has given me a unique vantage point that offers simultaneous views of the broad terrain of Yoga and the world of equity investment. I gradually began to notice that several roads connected these two seemingly disparate worlds.

I thought of all the seminars, workshops, and symposiums I had attended, and all the white papers I had read over the years on the subject of investment. I also weighed in the plethora of approaches, investment philosophies, media interactions, and perspectives on the subject.

The best minds in the world of investing agree that investor psychology is the key to creating great wealth. While we understand that the mind is one's biggest friend, it can also be one's biggest enemy; and that is very true in the world of equity investing. Having realised that there is no better guide to understanding, disciplining and harnessing the power of the mind than the Patanjali Yoga Sutra, it became clear that I had to write this book.

This book has been written as a guide for investors, both beginners and existing ones, on how they can make their money work for them and create phenomenal wealth by investing it wisely in the equity market, using the wisdom of ancient scriptures, mainly the Patanjali Yoga Sutra. I have also taken the help of other revered scriptures, including the Bhagavad Gita wherever necessary, to substantiate the fundamental Yoga concepts explained. In fact, Yoga vidya is much beyond Yoga sutras and bhagavad gita and I would urge the readers to go out and acquire more knowledge for their overall self development.

I firmly believe that if one endeavours to create wealth over the long term, then one cannot ignore equity as an asset class and must find ways to invest in equity either directly through stocks or indirectly through Mutual Funds. Therefore, the book provides a simple overview of the complex investment ecosystem and focuses primarily on equity as an asset class. Further, the book dives deep into the workings of the human mind and explains how it can be enriched with the insights of the Patanjali Yoga Sutra. This book explains 22 traits which affect the behaviour of an individual. Some of them are positive and hence, need to be strengthened while some of them are negative and therefore need to be minimized or stilled. The book also gives an insight into how the maestros of the investing world have consciously or unconsciously used these thought processes and philosophies, as substantiated by the ancient scriptures, to create immense wealth for themselves.

In essence, the book you hold invites all 'dhana-aarthis' or those who aim to create wealth to make it all happen with the timeless principles of Yoga investing.

Without further ado, let's dive deeper into the discipline of Yoga investing!

Module 1

Panchkleshas of Investing

तदासर्वाअवरणमलापेतस्यज्ञानस्याअनन्त्यात्ज्ञेयमल्पम्

Tadā sarva-āvaraṇa-malāpetasya jñānasya-ānantyāt jñeyamalpam

This (The culmination of the practice of Yoga) is a state of freedom where one knows all there is to be known.

– 4.31 Patanjali Yoga Sutra

Through the elimination of the veils of imperfection, one would encounter a state of limitless knowledge and may end up believing that there is scarcely anything left to be known.

The purpose of investment is to create and grow wealth. Yogic investing is a discipline that uses the insights of Yoga to help an investor create phenomenal wealth in the most efficient manner. Sound knowledge of one's mind as well as the equity market, works as a light on the path of wealth creation, whereas mental stability allows one to take rational investment decisions at opportune times.

A qualified civil engineer who knows the load-bearing capacity of a rickety bridge to be 100 kgs will not succumb to advice to drive across to the other side with his family. A Yogic investor will similarly not overexpose himself to risk, as he is armed with the necessary knowledge to take a rational investment decision. He also possesses the emotional stability that renders him immune to behaving like a member of a herd. A Yogic investor understands, analyses and makes rational decisions. He is not swayed by rumours, tips and hearsay and his sources of knowledge are sound and impeccable.

So, what is it that a Yogic investor possesses, which enables him to think more rationally than other investors? The answer, in the light of the Patanjali Yoga Sutra, is 'Panchakleshas' or five causes for sorrow. A Yogic investor weakens his Panchakleshas to a major degree whereas an ordinary investor is swayed by them. It is therefore imperative that we begin our journey into the world of

Yoga investing with an understanding of Panchakleshas and how they impact the investor's mind.

The Patanjali Yoga Sutra recognises the role played by ignorance in failure and the importance of knowledge in steering one to success. It is only in the light of knowledge that we can act with clarity. Every action performed in a state of ignorance exposes us to the danger of downfall.

Maharshi Patanjali, the author of the Yoga Sutra, explains how ignorance breeds a host of other causes for suffering in a short, simple and yet profound line:

अविद्याअस्मितारागद्वेषाभिनिवेशःक्लेशाः

Avidyā-Asmita-rāga-dveṣa-abhiniveśaḥ kleśāḥ

Lack of knowledge, ego, attachment, aversion and fear of loss are the causes for sorrow.

– 2.3 Patanjali Yoga Sutra

The Yoga Sutra identifies five causes for suffering called *Panchaklesha* i.e., *Pancha,* meaning number five in Sanskrit and *Kleshas,* meaning the causes for suffering. So, PanchaKlesha translates roughly into the five afflictions. As we proceed, we will learn that the very afflictions that are said to cause sorrow are also hurdles to be crossed before one becomes a successful equity investor. The discipline of Yoga loosens the grip of the Panchakleshas on the mind. Applied to the practice of wealth-creation or investment, the very same causes of sorrow comes in the way of making sound investment decisions. The Panchakleshas distort thinking and drive people to make irrational decisions. It is, therefore, imperative for the Yogic investor to overcome these Kleshas before operating in the market like a rational human being.

The five Kleshas

So, what are the five causes for affliction or Kleshas according to Patanjali?

- **Avidya (Ignorance)**
- **Asmita (Ego)**
- **Raga (Attachment)**
- **Dvesa (Aversion)**
- **Abhinivesha (Fear of loss)**

Avidya

Imagine an archer who is unable to judge the size, the position and the distance of the target due to the distorting spectacles over his eyes. What are the archer's chances of finding the mark? What are the chances of success for an investor who sets out to create wealth without understanding the market and studying its working with clarity?

In the state of *Avidya*, one takes blind shots at perceived targets and is lucky to find the mark sometimes. The odds of success for such a person is extremely low. What should be a game of chance actually turns into a gamble for the investor who is thus blinded or misled by ignorance.

Avidya or ignorance has been described as the root cause of all afflictions. It is Avidya that makes the ignorant compare equity investing with gambling. It is true that the markets are complex and constantly evolving and changing. This makes multiple outcomes possible for every investment situation. Once the light of *Vidya* clears the way, the equity market loses its mystery and its truths are laid bare before the eyes. The equity market disappoints people who do not invest their time, effort and money in acquiring knowledge of its working. No wonder, Avidya has been described as the mother of all Kleshas in the Yoga Sutra. There are largely two kinds of Avidya – lack of knowledge and wrong knowledge which will be detailed in the pages to follow.

The five Kleshas are often depicted as a tree. Avidya is the trunk of the tree, and the four other Kleshas sprout from it, as branches.

The Five Kleshas

ASMITA: EGO – THE SENSE OF 'I'

It is said that 'knowledge of ego is knowledge and ego of knowledge is ego'. It is important for an investor to differentiate between the two clear categories called 'facts' and 'opinions'. However, it is easy for a person with Avidya (ignorance) to confuse mere opinion with fact. It is ego or Asmita that convinces someone to believe that their unfounded opinion, rooted in Avidya, is actually a factual truth. It is, therefore, important to check at every point whether the research or opinion at hand is based on a brutally honest observation of the facts or merely an ill-founded opinion based on Avidya. The deeper the Avidya, the stronger is the delusion in the self or Asmita and greater the confusion between fact and opinion. The market is full of ignorant or half-learned investors who freely dispense advice to anyone who cares to listen. The tendency to give advice when it is not even sought, is a telling sign of Asmita.

As a to-do, one has to constantly ask oneself if a conclusion has emerged out of the 'scene' or the reality on the ground or is it sprouting from Asmita or ego rooted in Avidya? It is Asmita or ego rooted in Avidya that leads to misplaced and sentimental ideas like 'my investment', 'my sector', 'my price', or 'my investment style'. In other words, the market is the 'scenery', which operates independent of our ideas of 'I', 'me' and 'mine'. Those who operate from Avidya or delusion let their emotions get involved in the investing process and this leads to serious lapses in judgment.

'I know it all' is the defining characteristic of this Klesha. With such a deluded ego comes a bloated confidence that quickly turns into overconfidence. This is when a lot of disasters happen in the game of investment.

RAGA: ATTACHMENT

Raga is attachment or attraction. It is natural to be drawn to that which one finds attractive. One may ask why being attached or attracted to something should be considered a problem. And why is it a problem when it comes to investing? Patanjali says, a mis-guided self tends to make choices based on what has given it pleasure in the past. This can be dangerous as an investor should respond to an emerging situation on the merits of that specific situation and not on the basis of memory as every situation is unique. Raga also manifests itself as attachment towards a particular asset class or a specific option within an asset class.

Investors have a good chance of making money in a market that is moving northward even if their reasons for investing in a particular stock are not sound. Such a market masks one's failures easily. Buoyed by confidence from the experience, one may mistakenly believe that one has figured out the market. Such bull phases deepen Raga or attachment to pet theories, pet stocks and pet sectors by rewarding everyone including the ignorant.

In this ignorance we often hold on to stocks that give us good returns in the short-term, but lead to loss in the long-term. Raga or attachment will often compel people to stay invested in asset classes like gold or real estate that are past their prime despite evidence that clearly points out to the changed realities. Raga results in clouding of rational decision-making abilities. All Kleshas, including Raga, thin out when knowledge dawns upon the seeker. A Yogic investor can deal with Raga by ensuring that his investment decisions are guided solely by the latest data at hand and not by an emotional memory of or attachment to what used to be a good investment avenue or by mere opinions rooted in Asmita or ego.

DVESHA: AVERSION

Dvesha is aversion, the opposite of Raga. One may experience repulsion to the market, which is perceived to be painful. Because both Raga and Dvesha are rooted in ignorance, they make a person irrational. In an investor, Dvesha expresses itself as aversion to certain asset classes or within financial assets to stocks, sectors or investment theories. Dvesha or aversion, like Raga or attachment

thrives in the state of ignorance or Avidya. Dvesha is rooted in memory, like Raga. We fear or are repulsed by things that have brought us pain in the past. A person in ignorance acts not after one's Viveka (process of differentiating right from wrong) that has worked on the data at hand but on the basis of one's prejudices that have been characterised as Raga and Dvesha in the Yoga Sutra. It is important to note that Raga and Dvesha are but two sides of the same coin. Just as water disturbed by ripples does not reflect an object accurately, a mind disturbed by Raga and Dvesha cannot perceive an investment opportunity clearly. The answer, as pointed out earlier, is to ground oneself progressively in Vidya or knowledge. The equity market is no place for the emotionally unstable.

ABHINIVESHA: FEAR OF LOSS

Fear of change has also been termed as the 'fear of death' or Abhinivesha because all change demands that we unlearn and relearn. People cling to old ideas because they fear they would lose everything if they acted differently from the way they have always done. The investor who does not change in the face of contrary research because something is not aligned to a pet theory, is probably fearful of change. Abhinivesha is, therefore, equally the fear of losing everything. The fear of loss is a major barrier to healthy investing. Fear of loss may prevent one from recognising opportunities for creating wealth. Markets are volatile by nature. Share prices keep fluctuating and one may never get a linear return. However, knowledge of fundamentally strong equity investing concepts and patience to stick with it can help one minimise Abhinivesha or fear of loss and create long term wealth.

In conclusion, people in Avidya mistakenly believe that they know enough to operate in the market. It is Avidya or ignorance that gives birth to this 'I-know-it-all' attitude. The sense of self that springs from Avidya has been called Asmita or ego. Asmita is the ego or psyche or personality rooted in Avidya. All egos, psyches or personalities have likes and dislikes. The deeper one is in the state of Avidya, the more extreme are the likes and dislikes in a person. The likes manifest as attraction, which are called Raga. The dislikes are expressed as aversion and collectively called Dvesha. A mind in Avidya constantly oscillates between Raga and Dvesha. Such a mind steeped in ignorance develops a deluded sense of self-worth, which makes an individual act out of irrational likes and dislikes and fear of change as one would fear death. The answer, simply, is to acquire the right knowledge and act in the light of that knowledge.

Yoga is an attempt to weaken the hold of Kleshas or causes for suffering (Avidya, Asmita, Raga, Dvesha, Abhinivesha) over the mind so that it becomes still, like a mirror. In the context of investor psychology, these PanchaKleshas come in the way of investing optimally. Unless the mind is clear of suffering or Kleshas, one's investment portfolio is unlikely to be healthy. Let us take a deeper look at the art of weakening Kleshas along with some time-tested Yoga investment Mantras to help us along the path of wealth creation.

Chapter 1

Avidya

Avidya

अविद्या क्षेत्रमुत्तरेषाम् प्रसुप्ततनुविच्छिन्नोदाराणाम्

Avidya kṣetram-uttareṣām prasupta-tanu-vicchinn-odārāṇām

Ignorance is the source of all causes for sorrow or Kleshas.

– 2.4 Patanjali Yoga Sutra

While the Yoga Sutras speak of Avidya as the state of ignorance that all beings are born into. Our discussion in this book confines itself to ignorance or Avidya as it relates to investment behaviour. The ignorance that pertains to Avidya in an investor can be remedied by the acquisition of Vidya or knowledge. Avidya comes in the way of creation of wealth. It is probably the biggest reason for not investing optimally. From the perspective of investment, besides the fact that Vidya and Avidya (knowledge and ignorance) co-exist in every organism in varying degrees, there are largely two kinds of Avidya – lack of knowledge and wrong knowledge.

One may be said to possess wrong knowledge when one allocates most or all of one's investment in sub-optimal asset classes like fixed deposits, gold or real-estate, considering it as the best investment option for growing their wealth. As a result,

most of these investors fail to achieve significant inflation adjusted return or *'real returns'*.

The lack of knowledge of investment avenues leads one to invest on the basis of hearsay. People invest money in equity markets following tips from friends / relatives, expecting it to grow overnight. It has also been seen that people even take investment decisions based on 'tips' received on SMS or WhatsApp messages, without confirming the credentials of the source. When it comes to investing, we often squander our hard earned money impulsively in over leveraged companies and penny stocks without a background check on subjects like promoters, financials and valuations. When we make such an impulsive purchase decision, investment is reduced to a matter of chance like playing a lottery or gambling where our odds of getting it right shrink dramatically.

Now compare this to how you typically make a buying decision in other areas. When you decide to purchase a refrigerator worth Rs. 20,000, you take all efforts to understand its features and specifications like capacity, number of doors, etc. You also compare it with other make/models and read several reviews before making the purchase. Now, if we exercise such prudence while purchasing a relatively low cost product such as a refrigerator, should we not be willing to undertake more research before investing our hard earned money?

It is imperative that we invest enough hours in research before we commit hard-earned money to an investment avenue. The first step in this direction is understanding the available avenues for investment, their nature, scope and rate of returns.

Understanding various investment avenues

There exist many avenues for investment. One can invest in fixed deposits, bonds, gold, real estate, debt mutual funds, equity, etc. One should be aware of the pros and cons of investing in various asset classes and also understand the strengths of equity as an asset class.

Before we move to studying different asset classes, let us get familiar with another important concept of investing. The average Indian investor does not realise that the value of an investment is deteriorating over a stretch of time, as a result of inflation, which eats into one's hard earned wealth by reducing the value of money. Such investors are happy with the returns in percentage terms, usually single digit, and never question the proceeds. It is important that one understands the difference between nominal return and real return. Using an example to understand this, let's say someone earns 6% interest on a bank fixed deposit. This is the nominal return and the real return of the investment is actually the return expressed in terms of the money value minus inflation, i.e., say, 6% interest – 4% inflation = 2% real return.

Now, let us consider each of the options on the basis of the value they offer as investment opportunities.

As we go through the list, let us try to understand the right avenues/ instruments for our needs. Keep in mind that we don't have to pick just one. Successful investors are those who do not put all their eggs in one basket.

To start with, there are mainly two types of asset classes - physical assets and financial assets. Physical assets are those which can be felt/ touched; these give us a sense of their physical presence, e.g., real estate, gold/ other precious metals and art. In contrast, financial assets are those which one does not get to feel or touch, e.g., debt or equity instruments. Now, let us have a deeper look at various instruments available under each asset class.

PHYSICAL ASSETS

- **Real Estate:** Investment in a piece of land, e.g., agricultural land or plotted development or construction, either commercial or residential development, is termed as a real estate investment. The investment may (as in the case of agricultural produce or rent income from residential or commercial development) or may not (as in the case of plotted development) offer a regular income stream. Real estate generally acts as a hedge against inflation and the appreciation in capital value depends on its location.

- **Gold or other precious metals**: Gold as an investment is a store of value, influenced by inflation. It is not an income generating asset and is also consumed in the form of jewellery or gold coins.

FINANCIAL ASSETS

- **Debt Instruments:** Debt instruments offer a return in the form of a fixed regular stream of future income.

  - Fixed Deposit: It is a financial instrument offered by banks/ non-banking institutions which provide investors with higher interest rates compared to a regular savings deposit. The investment is locked for a specified time period.
  - Bond: It is a fixed income investment in which the investor lends to an entity for a specific period at a fixed or variable interest rate.
  - Non-Convertible Debentures: They are unsecured bonds that cannot be converted into a company's equity

on maturity. They usually offer higher interest rates compared to convertible debentures.

- Mutual Fund Debt schemes: Debt MFs mainly invest in a mix of debt or fixed income securities such as T-Bills, G-Secs, Corporate Bonds, etc. with an aim to generate regular income for investors.

— **Equity**: Equity is a fractional/part ownership of a business venture whether listed on exchanges or unlisted.

- **Mutual Fund Equity schemes**: MFs invest in the common equity stocks traded on exchanges with an aim to generate higher returns at limited risks.
- **Direct Equity / Common Stocks**: Investors can own equity shares directly and become partners in the business thereby sharing the risks and profits associated with the ownership.

On analyzing the performance of asset classes from a wealth creation perspective, it is found that FDs and bonds seldom give higher real returns (i.e., net returns taking inflation into account), gold is relatively unproductive in nature, in terms of absence of regular cash flows, and real estate is highly illiquid and is associated with an opaque market. One should avoid lopsided exposure to these asset classes in their portfolio. When compared with other asset classes, equities have reported higher returns over a 10–20 year scale or even a 100-year scale. Despite having to go through a number of recessionary phases between the years 1900–2000, time and again, global equities have returned more than double the returns, on an average per year, compared to bonds and cash (short term maturities).

Let us now dwell upon the advantages of equities in detail.

ADVANTAGES OF INVESTING IN EQUITIES

Fighting inflation: With each passing year, prices keep rising. Inflation eats into one's savings. Investments help one protect one's capital against price rises. A way to beat inflation is to park one's money in investments that offer returns that are higher than the rate of inflation. Time and again, equities have given the highest inflation adjusted rate of return over the long term.

Growth of Capital: It is important to identify the potential of assets to provide a return in the form of value appreciation, referred to as capital gains. It must be noted that unlike debt instruments the capital appreciation in equities is not linear in fashion but many times, lumpy in nature. This calls for patience, i.e., long term investment on the part of the investor, amidst inherent volatility in markets.

Large-cap stocks, also referred to as blue-chip stocks, can offer good returns coupled with reasonable safety, modest income and potential for capital growth in the long-term with an increase in corporate revenues and earnings. Investments in midcap and smallcap stocks offer higher potential for growth. However, the associated risk is also higher.

Tax minimisation: New rules have been laid down for equity investments from FY19 onwards; equity investments held for more than 12 months would attract capital gains tax of 10%. Dividends (less than Rs. 10 lakhs) are tax-free in the hands of the investors. With this development Equity Mutual Funds will also attract long term capital gains tax. However, an investor must understand that in case of debt or real estate, the tax charged is much higher.

Liquidity: Unlike Real Estate, listed equity stocks can be easily bought or sold on the stock exchanges instantly and the proceeds are settled within a time period of 2 market working days, excluding the transaction date.

Safety: The Indian equity market is regulated by the Securities & Exchange Board of India (SEBI). SEBI is a vigilant and strict regulator of equity markets. It protects the interest of the investors and promotes the development as well as regulates the equity market, thereby making the stock market a safe investment destination for investors.

Transparency: Equities are traded on stock exchanges like the NSE and BSE which ensure total transparency of trades made through an order matching mechanism. They also eliminate the counterparty risk by ensuring that both the buyer and seller honour their respective commitments.

Let us analyse the movement of the Sensex from 1979 to 2022. The period in our analysis is a 43 year long period, covering several bull and bear markets cycles. Let us also look at a comparison of returns of various asset classes.

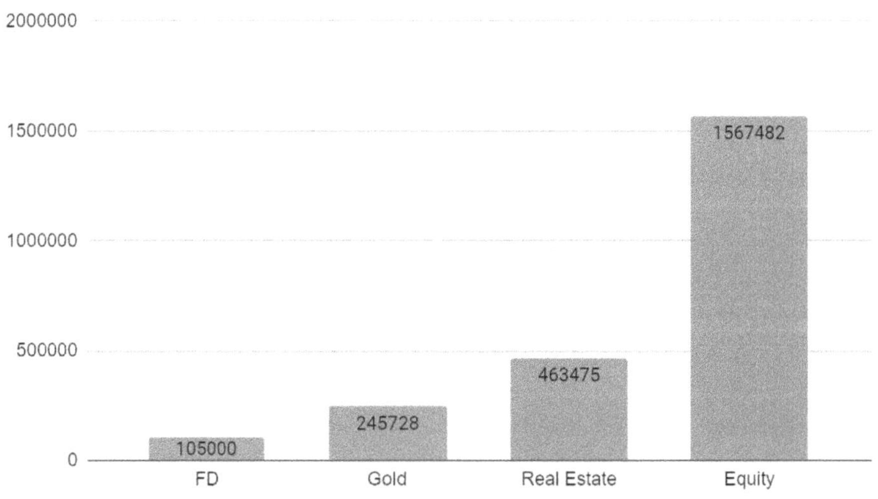

Rs 10,000 each invested in each of the four asset classes would have yielded different returns. As shown in the above representation Rs 10,000 invested in fixed deposits would have grown to Rs 1.05 lakh at the end of 30 years, yielding a CAGR of approximately 8%, while the corpus invested in gold would have returned around 10% every year. Real Estate was tad better than FD and gold offering ~13% returns over the same period while Equities outperformed the fixed deposits, gold and Real Estate by miles during the same period. While Real estate had yielded a return of 13% every year, equities grew at compounded by 18% CAGR in all these years. It must be noted, that though the difference in returns in there two asset classes i.e. Real Estate and Equities is barely 5 percentage points (500 bps), the absolute amount at the end of the period of investment is nearly four times for equity in comparison to real estate. Secondly, real estate investment is location specific and the returns may or may not be similar for all the pockets of investment. In the above representation we have assumed the investment returns for the micro market of Andheri, Mumbai which may differ for another city say, Delhi or Bangalore or Pune or Hyderabad.

The average annual return of the Sensex was 18% (for period between 1979 (when Sensex index was initiated at 100) till March 2023), which was far better than other asset classes. Thus, the risk return trade-off of equity versus other asset classes over a long investment horizon makes it a more attractive investment option for investors. It is therefore important for all to include equity in their investment portfolio, be it in the form of direct equity or through Mutual Funds.

The equity market has invariably proved itself to be the superior asset class, by creating wealth for people who have been patient with it. Unlike fixed income, whose returns are dependent

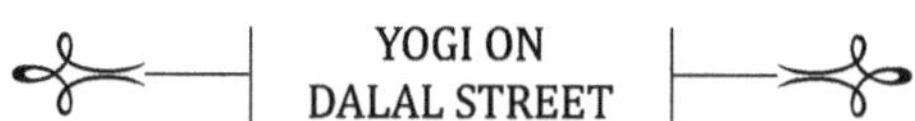

on changes in interest rate, the rate of return on equities is closely linked to the economy of the country. It has to be borne in mind that the economy of a country is generally northward looking since it is influenced exclusively by the enterprising nature of human beings.

BSE SENSEX SINCE INCEPTION

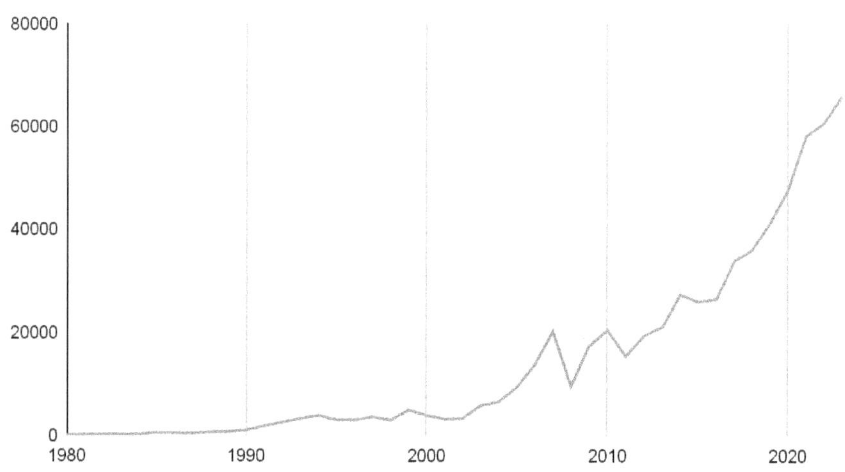

NSE NIFTY PERFORMANCE SINCE INCEPTION

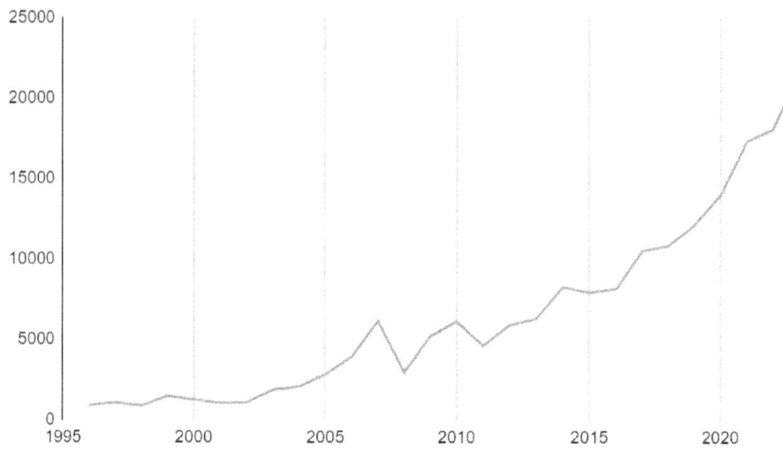

Sensex and Nifty offer clear evidence of huge returns for equity market investors. The complex interplay of forces that

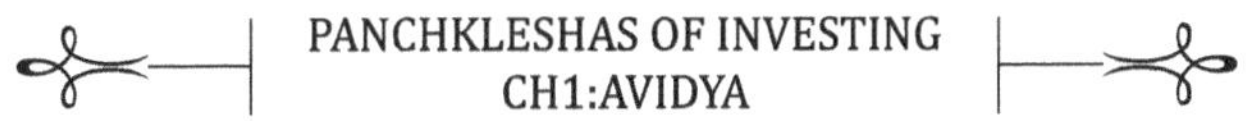

have led to growth in the past are available for those who wish to understand and predict changes in future. Having understood the impact of equity as an asset class, we can see that there exists a compelling rationale to invest in the Indian equity market. With strong demographics and positive economic indicators in India, the equity market is on a path to rise up and above, reigning expectations in the country. To understand this, one has to look at the India growth story.

The India growth story

The overall economy grew from USD 0.3 trillion in 1991 to USD 3.3 trillion in March 2023, with a majority of the gains coming in the last 15 years. In 2002, India was a USD 0.5 trillion economy; it crossed the USD 1 trillion mark in 2007, USD 2 trillion in 2014 and USD 3 trillion mark in 2019, despite global headwinds, like the Lehman crisis, the Eurozone debt crisis, the COVID Pandemic, etc., on account of its own inherent strength. The market capitalization of the Indian market has moved in tandem with its economic expansion. Currently, growing at upwards of 8% per annum, India is one of the fastest growing economies in the world.

As per the IMF, India is likely to become the 3rd largest economy by 2030, just after the US and China. Let us understand the strengths on the back of which the Indian economy is going to scale the coveted position.

1. **Favorable Demographic factors:** Demography can be broken into

    • **Large population:** India has the largest population in the world, which is growing at a rate of 0.81% p.a. The government is training a workforce of approximately 40 crore people.

- **Young population:** India has a very young population, around 50% of which is below the age of 25 and more than 65% below the age of 35.
- **Strong competitive positioning:** Competitive positioning refers to a set of features that help create value for a nation, compelling its growth. As per a latest report published by Ernst & Young, India's dependency ratio (number of dependents who are age 0–14 and age 65 above divided by population aged 15 to 64) is projected to reach its lowest value of 0.31, with a median age of 28 years.

  India entered its demographic window (period of time in a nation's **demographic** evolution when the proportion of population of working age group is particularly prominent) in 2010 and this window is expected to last until 2050. In contrast, Europe and the US are past their demographic window, whereas China's is on the verge of ending.

- **Foreign language skills:** India has the world's second largest English-speaking population. With around 20 to 25 crore people who speak English, India is said to have the largest population of 'fluent' English speakers, second only to the United States.
- **Growing but underutilized female workforce:** With India's workforce growing strong till 2050–2060, its female workforce participation rate, currently at 29.4%, has ample scope for growth and can triple from current levels, if the peak participation level, as reached by the West, i.e. 60–65%, is considered a benchmark.

2. **The second strong wave of reforms**: The reforms process which started in 1991 has picked up pace over the last couple of years. Reforms like demonetization, financial inclusion by implementing the Jan Dhan Yojana and direct benefit transfers (DBT) have strengthened the economy in terms of plugging the leakages in the system and removal of ghost recipients of subsidy benefits. As per the Global Findex report 2017, the number of bank account holders in the country has risen from 35 percent of adults in 2011 and 53 percent in 2014 to 80 percent in 2021. This, as per the report, is comparable to 80 percent of adults in China who have an account. This success can be attributed to progress being driven by the Jan Dhan Yojana policy, which has used the biometric ID, Aadhaar, to expand access to financial services. Implementation of GST has initiated a single tax across the nation, thus converting India into one market and the Insolvency & Bankruptcy Code has established a process to solve the pains in the banking system. In response to these moves, India has climbed to the 100th position in the Ease of Doing Business ranking and has targeted reaching the top 50 in the near future. Other reforms to reduce red-tape in administrative work, industrial workers policy, initiative to encourage SMEs & startups, etc., are in the pipeline, which will make India an investment friendly nation. The positive outcomes of the implemented measures are evident in the enhancement of both direct and indirect taxes, decreased government expenditure, ample liquidity in the banking system resulting in lower interest rates, and overall favorable macroeconomic conditions. All this will help the economy to grow at a faster pace in the years to come.

3. **Domestically driven economic expansion**: India is a fast growing emerging economy with 70% of its USD 3.5 trillion GDP (2022) driven by domestic factors and only 30% from exports. India is at the same inflection point at which the US was in the 1980s and China in the 1990s. In comparison with these developed and developing nations, India ranks far behind them in terms of infrastructure, per capita income, spending power, etc., which offer ample opportunities for the businesses to grow. To take an example, the penetration of cars in India is just 25.2 cars per 1000 people, which is around 90 for China and 908 for the US. The penetration for refrigerators in India is 33%, washing machines are around 13%, and air conditioners are merely 4.5%. Thus, there is ample scope for Indian automobiles, consumer durables and the consumer discretionary sector to grow on the back of the latent underlying demand.

To understand the quantum of opportunities that exists in India, let us compare the population statistics. India houses approximately 140 crore people of which more than 90 crore inhabit the rural areas. This is comparable to the entire population of Europe (74 crore). There are more than 40 crore middle class consumers, which is more than the entire population of the US. The share of youth in the population is upwards of 78 crore, which is more than the population of Brazil, Russia, Germany and UK. Thus, India is a consumption market equivalent to a few of the developing and developed economies clubbed together, in terms of population. At the same time, it is at the infancy of its growth on account of the low per capita income.

4. **Improved health of the economy:** Indian macro-economic parameters have improved significantly over

the last decade. Due to improving macros, India has emerged as the preferred investment destination among other emerging economies, like Brazil, China, Russia and South Africa. In fact, India is among the fastest growing large economies in the world with a GDP growth upwards of 8%.

From unsustainably high levels a decade ago, inflation, interest rates, the current and capital account deficits are now manageable:

- **Inflation on a downtrend:** Concerted efforts of the central bank continues to keep inflation in the range of 6%, protecting people from the effects of high cost thus improving their purchasing power.
- **Low Interest rate regime:** Low inflation also reflects into low interest rates thereby reducing the cost of borrowing for both the individual and corporate borrowers. This encourages individuals to buy durable goods, home and discretionary items like automobiles while the corporates invest into capacity expansion to suffice the rising demand.
- **Controlled twin deficit:** Both current account and fiscal deficit has been brought under control although the rise in crude oil prices has some upside risk for the current account deficit. Rise in tax collections following the implementation of GST (for indirect tax) and strict surveillance of direct tax collections would ensure improvement in tax collection, thereby containing the fiscal deficit.

Given these strengths, we can safely say that India is in a sweet spot of economic growth over the next couple of decades. Despite the positive outlook, the Indian middle class has so far remained away from equity as a preferred asset class. There are many reasons for traditional aversion to the equity markets, but the primary reason can be attributed to *Avidya* or *ignorance*. The ignorance about investment avenues and equity markets keeps people from turning their savings into wealth by using equity as an investment vehicle.

Keeping Avidya at bay

Making investments in the equity markets is not rocket science. It is all about putting to use what one observes around oneself. Do you know at what age investment guru Warren Buffett started investing? To put it verbatim: "I made my first investment at the age of 11. I was wasting my life till then." What does an 11-year-old boy understand about the equity market? How did he learn the knack of investing? In his childhood, he used to visit the supermarkets in his neighbourhood, sit there for hours watching people make purchases and make note of what they purchased. With these observations, he understood what was in demand and moving fast. He later applied his basic knowledge about products he observed people buying, to invest in companies that made and sold these products.

It is as simple as that.

If one looks carefully, one will notice how the world is rapidly changing. Small 'mom and pop' *kirana* shops are giving way to supermarkets. There's no need to visit various shops for groceries, bakery products, fruits, vegetables, and clothes anymore. All these items are conveniently accessible in one place, within a comfortable, air-conditioned environment. We love shopping in supermarkets. This is not only because of the discounts offered but also due to the convenience, ambience and the wide range of options. The

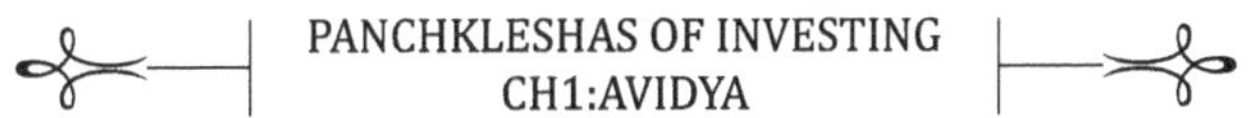

urban shopper, buoyed by increased purchasing power, is flocking to malls and supermarkets. More people are buying 2-wheelers or cars or SUVs than ever before. Consumer durables like refrigerators, washing machines, electronic gadgets, branded garments and clothing are flying off the shelves. Indians are watching movies in multiplexes, holidaying in destinations like Switzerland, Bali and Paris.

If one studies the 10-year revenue and earnings of the companies producing these goods and services and tries to correlate them with their share prices over the last 10–15 years, one will notice a positive correlation. Growth in the demand for these products and services has pushed share prices of companies that produce them upwards.

Take the example of Gillette India, a manufacturer of quality shaving paraphernalia. In 2001, the stock price of the company stood between Rs 200 and Rs 300. The current price has crossed Rs 6,800. In hindsight, considering the superior quality of Gillette products, its positioning as a premium brand, the company's international standing and the centrality of shaving in male grooming, it is not surprising that the shares of Gillette have seen such robust appreciation in value.

By extension, generating wealth in the future simply requires identifying comparable opportunities today, conducting a comprehensive analysis, and making informed investments. It is important to be convinced about the business potential of the company one invests in and to arrive at a conservative estimate of what one expects it to earn over the next couple of years. Armed with this data, one needs to have the mental strength to stay invested through the rough patches before the share price reaches the expected value because highs and lows are normal in a market.

Above all, one has to undertake due diligence of the target investment, before committing resources to it. One has to acquire actionable intelligence on the target company.

How?

All companies listed on the exchange are legally mandated to disclose information like balance sheets, profit and loss statements, etc. In fact, brokerage houses provide a wealth of information about the stock right from financials to key ratios. Therefore, if one wants to access information about a stock, it is readily available if one looks at the right places.

So, does that mean that in order to participate in equity, one must fully understand and research stocks? The answer is an emphatic NO! Even those who are unable to research a stock can participate in equity markets through three routes:

1. Exchange Traded Funds (ETFs)
2. Mutual fund schemes
3. Advice from reputed brokerage firms

As one moves from option 1 to option 3, the degree of risk increases, as does the probability of a higher potential return. In essence, before one invests in equities, one should spend some time on gathering actionable knowledge on the company behind the stock. A simple advice would be to invest only when you are convinced, beyond a doubt, about the company's future.

Conclusion

Given the fact that India is a great investment story and equity has been the biggest wealth creator, one must find ways to participate in equity markets, directly or indirectly. However, you should not ignore equity as an asset class. Having understood the benefits of

equity investment and its superiority among all the asset classes in terms of returns over the long term, it should be the natural choice of investment for individuals to take care of their long term investment goals. Choose the right companies, make investments wisely, on the basis of meticulous and actionable research, so that the investing process is based on Vidya or knowledge and not reduced into a hit-or-miss gamble.

Minimising Avidya by the knowledge of identifying the right company at the right price is what is required to make money in the stock market. If one stays invested for the long term, equity investments, either directly in stocks or through the mutual fund route, will surely provide significant real returns and create wealth. Long term investment minimizes risks associated with owning equities even if it becomes a disproportionately high part of one's portfolio.

Chapter 2

Asmita

Asmita: Ego

दृग्दर्शनशक्त्योरेकात्मतेवास्मिता ॥

Drig-darshana-shaktyor-eka-atmata-eva-Asmita

Ego (Asmita) is to perceive the seer and the seen as one.

– 2.6 Patanjali Yoga Sutra

The Yoga Sutras tell us that Asmita or ego is the mistaking of the seer with the seen. For example, we all have witnessed the sunset, but in fact, the sun never sets. It is the rotation of the earth, which makes it appear that the sun is going down. Therefore, what the seer believes to be true from their perspective may not be the truth in its entirety or may not be true at all. Backed by Avidya of planetary rotation, one may conclude or be in the ego that the earth is the centre of the universe and that the sun sets for the earth. Therefore, it is ego or Asmita that causes an investor to confuse the 'seer' or the facts with the 'seen' or opinion based on varying degrees of Avidya or ignorance. Such egos expand furiously during good markets, which, the wise say, make for bad teachers. Good markets or bull phases create money for investors and traders but it is the bad markets or bear phases that teach one to be a wise investor or trader. The equity market is full of self-proclaimed

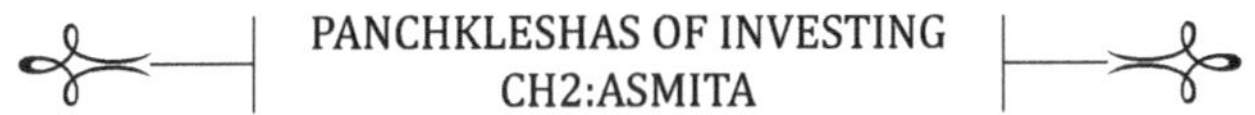

experts who casually throw in an 'I told you so' every time the market shoots northwards during a bull phase. In a typically good market any wild guess is likely to be on the mark. However, it is only during the lull period that the art of stock picking counts as only a few stocks manage to outperform the general trend despite the reigning pessimism.

The 'I know it all' ego is born and nurtured typically during bull markets when even stocks randomly picked by investors/traders are rewarded by the market with profits. This is dangerous because it breeds a false sense of superiority in amateurs who mistakenly think they have figured it out. Such unfounded optimism makes one complacent and blinds one to market signals, facts and trends. It is usual for such a person to be enamored by dangerous rumours often spread by clueless friends or colleagues who point out stocks that are supposedly guaranteed to deliver stupendous returns overnight.

A trader in the thrall of Asmita tends to be overconfident and ends up conducting more trades than less-confident counterparts. Such investors do so because they tend to believe that they are better than others at choosing the best stocks. They are also certain that they know the best time to enter or exit a position. For every trader, there could come a time when it becomes unclear whether they are trading to make money or to prove themselves right.

This is when disaster strikes.

The Yogic investor is constantly on guard for any signs of overconfidence within. Bragging about one's short-term investment performance is one sure sign to watch out for. A wise investor knows that one has to apply the brakes when the signs of overconfidence become visible. One has to perpetually be in fact-finding mode and never succumb to speculation. When someone offers a 'tip', one should always investigate; one should keep asking till all doubts vanish. Over time, one is likely to realise that most of such statements are little more than gossip or rumour. Even when a rationale is furnished in support of the 'tip', it is always prudent to undertake independent investigation on one's own before making an investment.

Ego is a double-edged sword. It not only lulls us into believing 'I know it all', which is but a step away from the 'I cannot be wrong' syndrome. Once one enters a stock believing 'I know it all' and the stock goes down-hill, it's hard to admit that one has made a mistake. In such situations, there is an unwillingness to sell the stocks at a loss because moving in that direction would prove that one has miscalculated. This admission of fallibility does not rest well with a bloated ego, which will often blind people to the weak fundamentals of a stock. Even after the market punishes sloppy investment behaviour, people in the hold of Asmita continue clinging to loss-making investments. The 'I cannot be wrong' attitude magnifies their losses, which can be cut easily if one is not emotionally involved in the process. Those stuck in such a situation are said to be value trapped. Getting attached to such an investment, despite clear signals from the market that demand quick surgical action, is a sure route to rapid wealth erosion.

Value traps

A value trap is a situation where the value of a stock appears to be a bargain when it is actually not. It is called a trap because one is deceived into buying a stock as it appears to be a bargain, when the 'real' value of the said stock is even lower. More often than not, value traps are a sign that the fundamentals of a company are changing adversely, or it can also point towards severe headwinds facing a business. Following is an example of a sector, which has seen a severe downfall after the 2008 economic crisis:

During the 2007–08 property boom, the real estate sector pursued rampant expansion plans, buying land to set up homes, malls and offices in major cities by taking a huge amount of debt. The players had also begun diversifying into unrelated areas. Post the infamous 2008 financial crisis, which had its epicentre in the US, the Indian economy slowed down. It led to the property market losing its steam, and the equity market going into a free fall. In addition to the debt on the books, many companies had pledged a part of their promoters' holding. And then the selling spree started as the outlook for the sector, in general, turned grim. To reduce their debt, companies began offloading some of their assets, particularly the non-core ones. The bearish phase in the sector was aggravated as some players offloaded pledged shares held by the financial institutions. By 2016, the whole sector was trading at a fraction of the market cap compared to the peak market cap witnessed in late 2007. But post COVID this sector has started growing bit by bit but still has not been able to reach the all time high scores.

Investors, who invested in the sector, overlooking the change in the fundamentals during its downfall, thinking that they were getting good value at a cheap price, found themselves stuck in a value trap. Typically, Asmita or ego does not let investors cut losses at such times. There are also investors who start accumulating stocks during this phase, thinking incorrectly that despite paying more they will manage to arrive at a lower average buy price in the final reckoning.

S&P BSE REALTY INDEX (from July, 2007 to Jan, 2024)

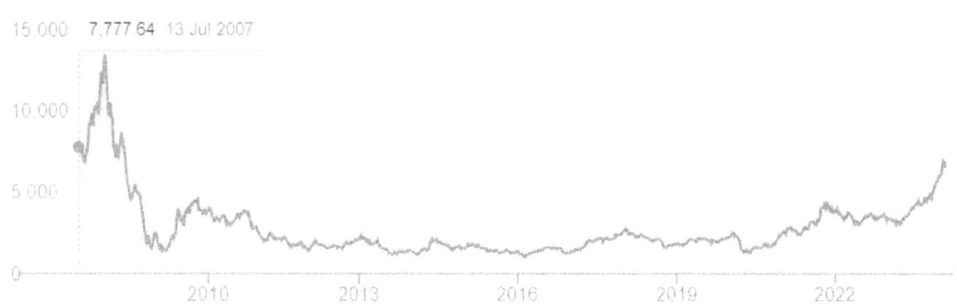

Identifying a value trap is tricky. It is difficult to make out whether what one is getting is a bargain or one is, in fact, walking into a value trap. The answer of course is to keep ego aside and study the fundamentals and market dynamics. If it becomes clear that it is a trap, it is advisable to exit a stock with minimal losses rather than carrying a truck load along due to Asmita.

How to avoid value traps

As an investor, one is not just investing in a stock, one is investing in a business. It follows that one has to understand the business one is investing in. If one is investing in an unknown business, it is like shooting in the dark. There are high chances of entering a value trap if one is not vigilant. Only after conducting proper due diligence, does one gain an accurate estimation of the strengths and weaknesses of a company. It is important to understand the past, the current environment and probable future prospects of a business before one invests in it. Once this knowledge has been acquired, it is easy to ascertain the potential of a target investment.

Only after the target investment has been thoroughly researched, one is able to make an informed decision about the company. This is

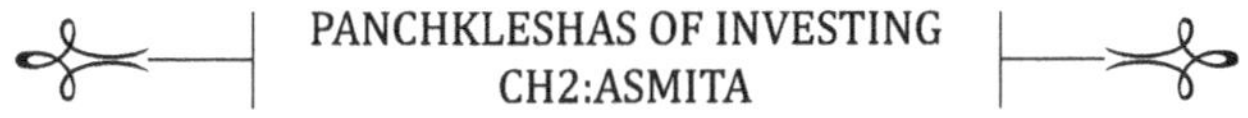

the key to arresting overconfident thinking at any point during the course of the investment.

Even if the business is one which one understands, the following parameters have to be considered before investing:

Valuation: A stock price that is highly undervalued in comparison with stocks of other companies in the same business should make one tread with caution. The low value may be a warning sign. One is advised to undertake thorough scrutiny of the company's business plan, financial performance and management practices. One must understand that past earnings have little effect on the future price of an investment. Undervaluation of a stock (or a sharp price correction) should not be the sole reason for investment. Dive Deep!

Business plan: Avoid companies that have business plans that are too complicated to understand or hard to explain. Keep away also from companies that are unable to make profits. A business should have good entry barriers. If a product or service can be offered by many players in the market, or finds itself on the verge of being outdated by new technologies, it is unlikely to give healthy returns. Technological obsolescence is a common misfortune that has struck several otherwise robust businesses.

Management: The management of a company is responsible for steering the business. It is imperative that the management has the highest levels of integrity, intelligence and energy. If it cannot be trusted, the companies run by it may not be worth investing in.

Debt on the balance sheet: High debt can cause problems with liquidity and solvency. It can sink a company with an otherwise good business plan. As we saw in the case of the real estate sector, highly leveraged companies have less leeway for making mistakes and overcoming obstacles, and are therefore the first to be punished when things go wrong. One should avoid investing in highly indebted companies.

Sustainable competitive advantages: Businesses that lack strategic advantages, which help them overcome obstacles like heavy regulations or tough competition can lose their ability to survive or compete in the long run.

Pro tip: Figure out if the company you intend to invest in has the ability to stay ahead of the competition. Check if the company is a market leader.

- Does it possess pricing power?
- Is it able to leverage economies of scale?
- Does it have popular brands under its umbrella?
- Are its production processes cost efficient?
- Does the management style reflect a clear vision?

Without one or more of these advantages, the sustainability of the entire enterprise may suffer in the long run. The above mentioned checklist should be strictly adhered to in order to keep oneself from getting engulfed into a value trap.

Keeping Asmita at bay

Avoiding the 'I cannot be wrong', which is also the 'I know it all' syndrome is the first step to ensuring that one keeps Asmita at bay. Few rules, if followed strictly, would prevent an investor from falling into the self-laid trap of developing overconfidence or ego:

Define an investment style - short-term or long-term - and stick to it. Discipline is the key to success even for a day trader. Adhering to strict stop losses prevents excessive erosion of investment when the trade goes wrong. While entering a trade, one should be clear about how much loss one is willing to bear. Ideally, one should never mix a trading portfolio with an investment portfolio. Remember, the equity market does not reward the smartest but the most disciplined and patient.

Do not hold on to losses while exiting the profit making ideas: Many times, a long-term investment is a short term trade gone wrong. When markets turn volatile, the jittery investors generally book profit on the profit making ideas and hold on to the loss making trades. Instead, if one encounters a situation where one has to sell a part of the holding/ portfolio, one must look at what one should still be buying (maybe due to cheap valuations) instead of looking at the profit or loss made in the earlier trades/ investments.

Conclusion

Perhaps the best tried and tested advice for investors stepping into the equity market is to avoid trying to outsmart the markets and instead work to outsmart themselves. One should remember to leave their ego aside before entering the equity market. We have no control over the market; we can only control ourselves. The Mantra to negate the ill-effects of Asmita/ego is to 'stay humble and ask for directions'. Learning is a never ending process. There should be no hesitation in seeking expert advice from reputed brokerage firms to validate one's views or rely on the expertise of fund managers of reputed Mutual Funds houses to manage one's money. Take decisions rationally as the path of logic is the path of the Yogic investor.

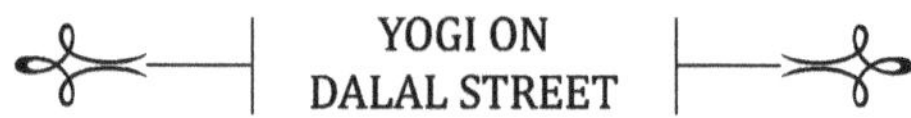

Chapter 3

Raga

RAGA: ATTACHMENT

सुखानुशयीरागः ॥

Sukha anushayi Raga

Attraction to a pleasant experience results in craving.

– 2.7 Patanjali Yoga Sutra

As we know, ignorance or Avidya is natural to all beings. The ego sprouts out of this state of existential ignorance. Such an ego rooted in Avidya has been described as Asmita in the Yoga Sutra, as we now know. The 'I' in the 'I-know-it-all' of Asmita experiences attachment or Raga to things that have given pleasure in the past and aversion or Dvesha to things that have given pain in the past.

45-year-old Rajesh still rides his old scooter. He spends a lot of time and energy repairing it even though the scooter has poor mileage, lacks performance and features. There are now better versions of lighter and gearless scooters available in the market. His rationale is that his scooter has emotional value attached to it. Rajesh's rather expensive attachment to his scooter is surprising and illogical. However, Rajesh is still not willing to give up his emotional attachment or Raga for his old scooter.

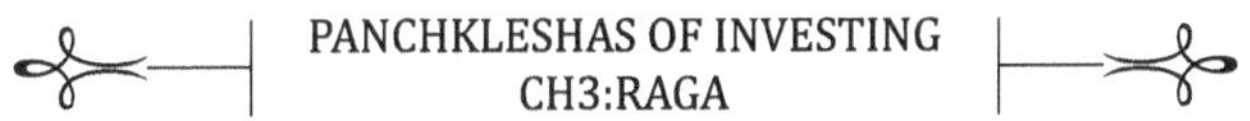

When seen from the perspective of investment, ignorance or Avidya of the market dynamics deludes people into believing that they are experts (Asmita or false sense of self), which then expresses itself as Raga (attachment) to stocks that have yielded profit in the past and Dvesha (aversion) to asset classes that are perceived either too risky or those that have rendered losses in the past. Behavioral Finance describes this bias which leads individuals to value an owned object higher than it actually is as '*endowment effect*'. In this section, we examine the role of Raga in investment behaviour and how it can be overcome through the dispelling of Avidya or ignorance.

Raga to an asset class or within an asset class (for e.g. to a particular stock within equity as an asset class) is a Klesha that takes tremendous effort to subdue. Some investors get emotionally attached to a particular asset class and sink all their savings in it. Gold and real-estate attract the lion's share of such savings. There are also investors in the equity market who get attached to one or two particular sectors due to emotional reasons. One must be wary of one's emotions as they may distract one from thinking rationally. Favouring a particular asset class or sector/ stock just because one likes it personally increases portfolio concentration risk. In case the asset class or stock goes through a downturn or a negative cycle, one runs the risk of substantial wealth erosion.

In the world of investing, attachment can be of 2 types:

- Attachment towards a particular asset class
- Attachment to a specific option within an asset class

Attachment to a traditional asset class like fixed deposits, real-estate or gold is very common. Just because we know more about a particular asset class or the fact that the asset has given us good returns in the past should not deter us from exploring better options. The biggest risk one can ever take is to not take any risk at all. One has to be willing to dive deep before a sunken treasure is discovered.

The primary aim of investment is wealth creation. It is therefore imperative for the investment to beat inflation by a wide margin so one benefits in the form of real returns. Traditional forms of investment like fixed income and gold fail to beat inflation by a margin and barely create any real return. Equity investments, on the other hand, have consistently created wealth over the long term.

Returns on fixed income instruments more or less mirror the rate of inflation. Effectively, the returns in 'real' terms from fixed income instruments are a paltry (2%-3% over the inflation) or even negative at times. There are different types of fixed income securities like Government bonds, recurring deposits, fixed deposits, mutual fund debt scheme, company deposits etc. A majority of these instruments, more or less, offer 'real' returns in low single digits. The only virtue of these investments is that the danger of default is minimal. Hence, if safety isn't one's only priority, one must be mindful of the impact of inflation on their investments. If one's goal is to build wealth for the future, a bond that pays real returns in low single digits isn't going to help.

As an asset class, gold is seen as a hedge against inflation in developed markets. For investors in developing markets, gold acts as a hedge against currency depreciation. Over an extended stretch of time, the value of gold has not appreciated in real terms. Physical gold pays neither dividend or interest. Instead, in the form of jewelry, it comes with the disadvantage of higher premium in the

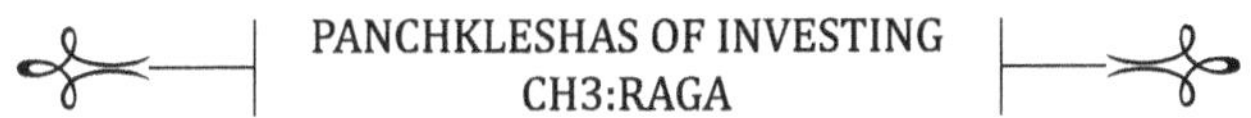

form of making charges and maintenance costs such as safety vaults or bank lockers. Also, due to the impurity risk and making charges, the resale value may not be at prevailing market prices. Therefore, if at all one wants to invest in gold, it should be through the electronic medium in the form of e-Gold or Gold ETFs that can be bought and sold on the exchange, like any stock, without having associated risks of purity, safety and liquidity. Further, if one wants to buy gold as an investment, one can look at Sovereign Gold bonds too, which offer some return, though very low.

For a retail investor looking at an exposure to real estate, projects in areas expected to emerge as the next residential or business hubs may be attractive investment opportunities. Most people think that an advantage of investing in real estate is that one can buy and sell at any time. However, the fact is that transaction costs in real estate, like brokerage and stamp duty, and the difference in the buying and selling prices due to illiquidity, creates an immediate negative return. Since many people buy real estate through the home loan route, the cost is further pushed northwards due to the burden of interest on EMIs. Also, real estate requires an outflow in the form of maintenance charges and repair costs. The possible inflows, in the form of residential rental yields, in India are poor and mostly in the range of 1.5 to 2%. A common misconception is that real estate is not affected by business cycles. Moreover, the performance of real estate is location specific and it is difficult for a retail investor to have a diversified portfolio in real estate as it requires huge investments. Overall, the Real Estate market is largely opaque in nature.

If we factor inflation into our investment calculations, equity as a class emerges as a clear winner due to its ability to beat inflation by a wide margin, despite volatility in the markets.

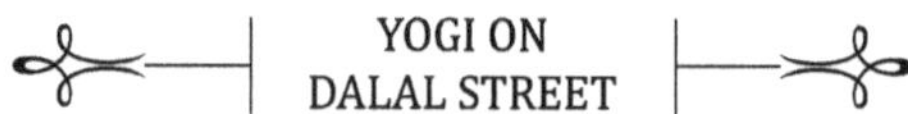

Of course, the investment has to be long term, say 3 to 5 years or maybe more. The domestic index, the Sensex has multiplied 710X plus since its inception 44 years ago, in 1979, which gives us a compounded annual growth rate of 16% till December 2023. Equities offer the magic of compounding, which enables the investment to multiply over the years. To conclude, equities beat other classes in nominal terms despite the volatility involved. Hence, if one aims to create wealth, equity investment is the way to go, in the long term.

There is indeed the risk of short term market fluctuations, which renders equity riskier than fixed income investments. However, as the holding period grows, the risk decreases, while the compounded real returns improve significantly.

People have a great attachment to physical assets, like gold and real estate, as they can feel and see them. Both these physical assets are difficult to manage and maintain. The returns gained are relatively low too. Investors attached to these assets often shy away from diversifying into other asset classes despite the chances of earning substantially better returns.

Attachment to a specific option within an asset class can also be seen among investors. For instance, some people like to invest in gold only through jewellery or some like to invest in real-estate only in a particular area. Similarly, some equity investors develop an affinity to sectors or stocks which have given them good returns in the past. It has been seen that investors caught in the mesh of the 'Raga' stay invested despite a situation where their expectations are belied by the market. Such is their attachment to the sector that they refuse to factor the severe headwinds blowing in the sector into their calculations. Turning a blind eye to the changing investment

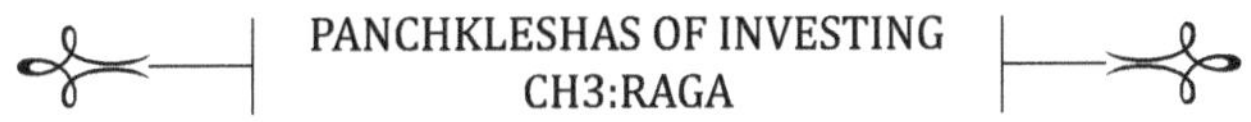

landscape is extremely dangerous. It is a sure road to losing one's wealth.

Markets are cyclical in nature. Sectors that did well in the past may or may not deliver great returns in the future while underperforming sectors may emerge as winners. Equity markets reward the growth associated with the sector or the industry, hence the sector that will drive the markets will keep changing. As the sector matures, the growth plateaus and so do the valuations. Let us look at examples of two industries that had delivered in the past but could not continue on the same growth trajectory in the future:

Attachment to a stock has been commonly found among retail investors, especially when they initiate their investments in equity. To start with, they identify low priced stocks, i.e. stocks available at low denominations, say below Rs 100 or Rs 50, irrespective of the valuations. The rationale for identifying a low priced stock is that they can buy a larger quantity for a specified amount of corpus invested. Instead, it is wise to be on the lookout for an undervalued stock with growth potential, irrespective of the price it is currently trading at.

Attachment is also seen among speculative investors.

Such investors undertake little or no research before allowing themselves to be enamored by hearsay and hold on to a stock despite continuous earnings downgrades. Some investors feel that as long as they have not sold out their loss making holdings, they have not booked losses. They fail to take into account the opportunity cost associated with an investment. Opportunity cost in this case is the returns they give up, had they decided to sell the loss making stock and buy the second best investment. They stay on with their

paper losses despite a change in the investment landscape. It is not surprising to see investors holding on to shares of companies that have faded away with the passage of time due to a loss of business and competitive advantage, over leveraging, and compromise in promoter integrity.

Keeping Raga at bay

As explained above, each asset class has its own shortcomings and thus, on its own, would not suffice as a strong investment opportunity. A hundred percent exposure to any one asset class, be it gold or real estate, will lead to returns that might not beat inflation or even cause a loss in principal investment. It is essential for individuals to diversify their investments across asset classes.

Exposure to a specific option within an asset class is also detrimental to the health of an investment. Focusing on equities, investors influenced by Raga may not be able to get their mind off a particular sell-price target (the anticipated price at which the investor intends to sell a particular stock). They continue to hold on to the stock despite new information that indicates that the investment landscape has shifted significantly. They become stuck and choose to ride markets to the bottom as they cannot let go of what they think the price 'should' be. A short-term trader ends up becoming a long-term investor due to an attachment or anchoring to the price. Investment decisions should be repeatedly reviewed on the basis of business cycles, management quality and investment themes. Getting fixated on a specific price is never a good idea. Any change in the parameters should qualify for a relook at the investment. If there are no fundamental reasons for one to hold the stock, it is better to sell,

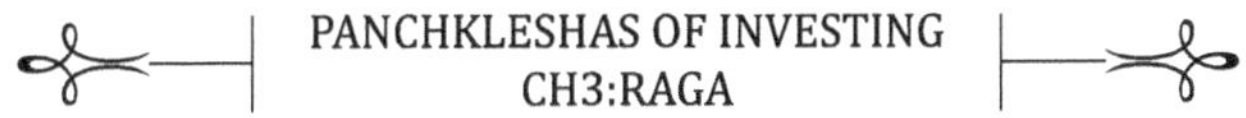

take a capital loss and reinvest the money in another idea. This approach enables the investor to make profits and recover losses made in the earlier investment.

Diversification

For an investor planning for the long-term, diversification is the best strategy. One should allocate one's investments across various asset classes. Specifically within financial asset classes, diversify across sectors and stocks. Just like consuming a balanced diet is important to stay healthy, keeping a balanced asset allocation in a portfolio is vital for the health of one's portfolio. Diversification maximises returns by minimising the risk.

The importance of diversification may be understood with the help of an example of two people who have decided to invest the same amount of money but with an allocation in different asset classes.

Consider Mr. A who has Rs. 1,00,000 in his account and decides to invest in a mix of asset classes, say Rs. 33,333 in Fixed Deposits or MF Debt schemes, Rs. 33,333 in direct equity/equity mutual funds and Rs. 33,333 in Gold. While Mr. B, who also has Rs. 1,00,000 in his account decides to invest the entire amount in gold.

The computations have been done over the period starting 1 April, 2017 to 31 March, 2022. Since the market was more volatile than usual during this period due to the global pandemic, we will be able to understand the benefits of diversification better.

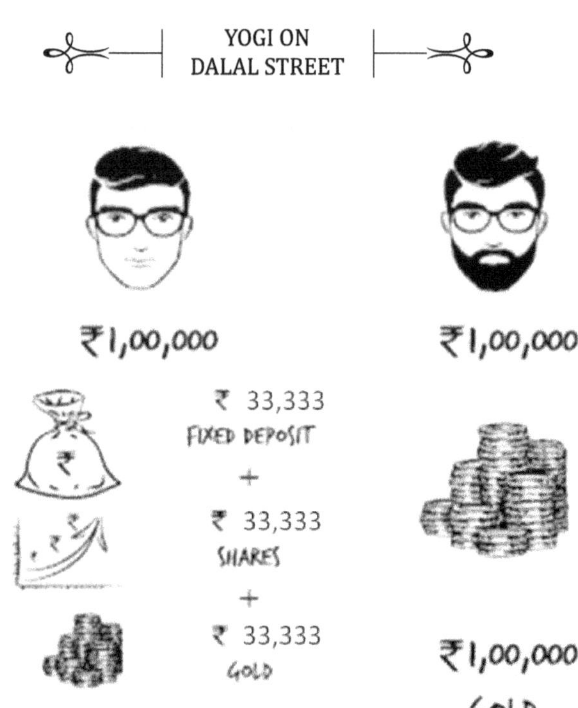

After 5 years, both decide to evaluate the returns they have earned on their investments.

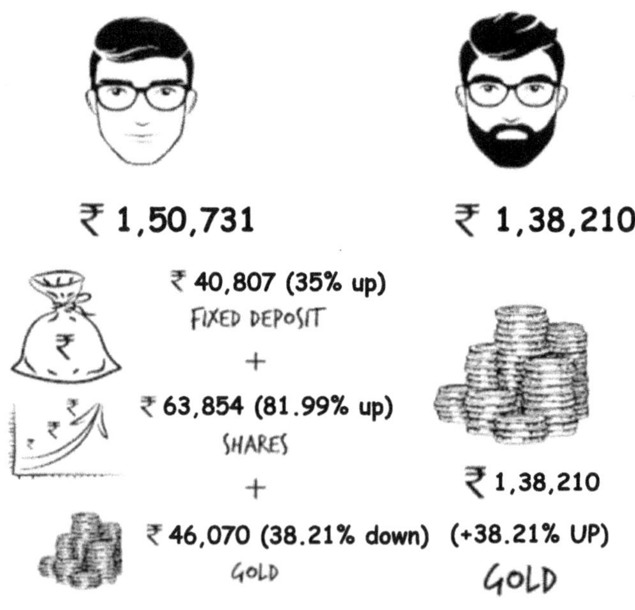

Mr. A earns a return of 38% on his investment with his portfolio value increasing to Rs. 1.38 lakh (approx.), whereas, Mr. B earns a return of about 51% on his investment, thus his principal amount has risen to Rs. 1.51 lakh (approx).

As we can see, Mr. A invested in different asset classes and could earn a higher return. Mr. B experienced loss of opportunity by investing everything in gold.

Investors who adopt the approach of diversification end up earning higher returns not just during outlier events, but in the absence of such events. The example illustrates how diversification helps in protecting the portfolio from extreme downsides by compensating for the underperformance of one asset class with the outperformance of other asset classes, thereby reducing risk substantially. This is because diversifying across asset classes makes one's portfolio immune to market cycles and increases the probability of higher returns by minimising risk. Since all asset classes do not react in the same way at any given point in time to market events and business cycles, this limits the downside to the portfolio.

Diversification according to risk profile

It is essential to know how one can diversify one's investments.

Diversification depends on 3 things:

1. Risk   Internal to the Asset
2. Return
3. Investment horizon   Internal to the Investor

While the risk and return are inherent to the different asset classes, we must decide the investment horizon for which we are looking to invest, i.e. short term or long term. A correct diversification strategy would be one which enables us to achieve an optimum trade-off between these 3 parameters.

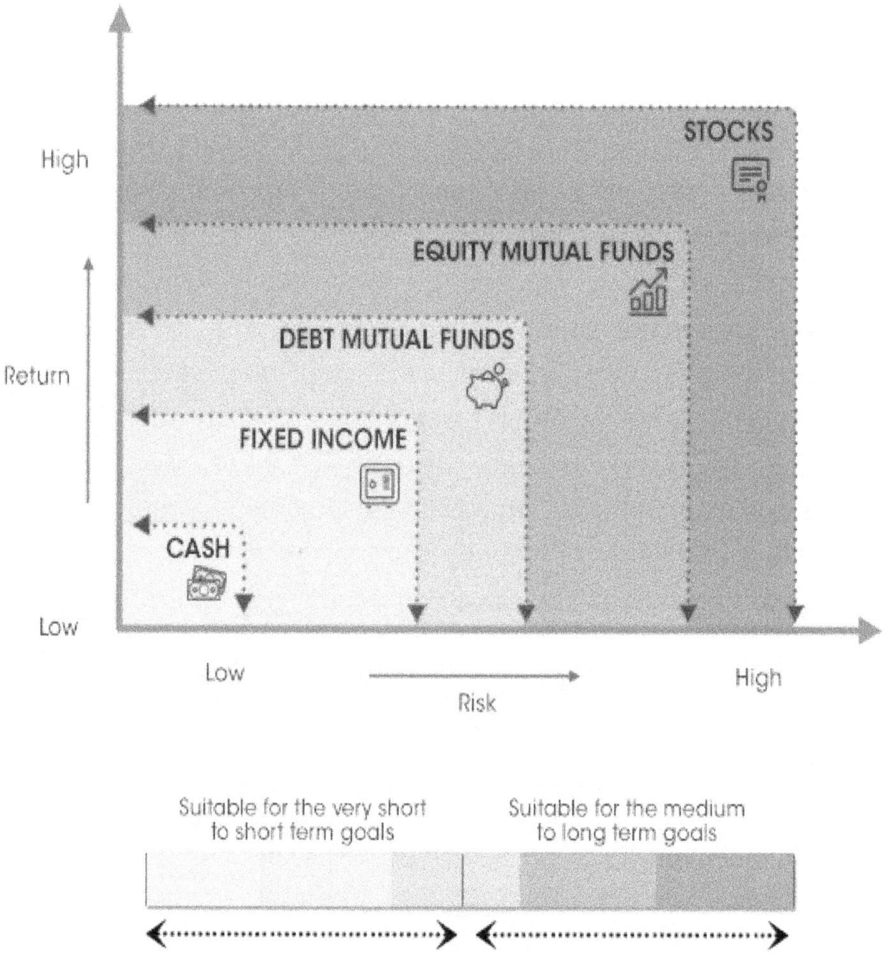

The above chart will help us identify the risk of each asset class versus its return.

Assets which involve least risk but at the same time give relatively low returns include cash and fixed income.

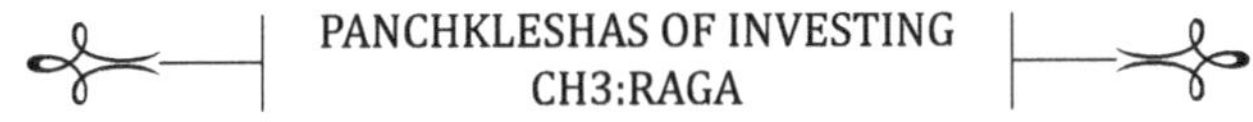

Assets which offer high return but are associated with relatively more risk include stocks and equity mutual funds.

Taking the above parameters into consideration, we align them with our internal parameters and arrive at our investment horizon.

In case we require protection of capital and have short term money requirements, our portfolio should include a high percentage of cash and fixed income.

For growth of capital as well as wealth creation over the longer term, our portfolio should have equity mutual funds and stocks.

Conclusion

In order to beat Raga, it is important that one not only diversifies among asset classes as a whole, but also diversifies within a particular asset class, across various types of instruments. For example, in the case of stocks, diversify based on size – large cap, mid cap and small cap. While large caps are low-risk investments, small cap stocks carry high-risk. Always remember to diversify investments through asset allocation. This is the best way to ensure predictability of returns as and when one asset class or a subset of that particular asset class falls, there are others to compensate for the loss.

Chapter 4

Dvesha

DVESHA: AVERSION

दुःखानुशयी द्वेषः

Duḥkha-anuśayī dveṣaḥ

Dvesha is pain caused by contact, thought or proximity of that which one is repulsed by.

– 2.8 Patanjali Yoga Sutra

Patanjali lists aversion as a trait inherent in Asmita (ego) along with Raga (attachment). Aversion is natural to all beings. However, humans alone have the ability to think, which offers them an opportunity to rise above their aversions. In Yoga, Dvesha is considered to be one of the four causes for sorrow because a person with strong aversions becomes temporarily irrational, which pushes them towards decisions that are harmful. For example, we come across a lot of cases of road accidents in the media which may cause one to have an unpleasant experience, but it would be irrational to associate travelling with accidents alone. The news itself should not deter someone from travelling by vehicles. Similarly, investors cannot afford to suspend their Viveka or ability to differentiate right from wrong. A Yogic investor has to therefore watch out for the rising of Dvesha in the mind, which is more often than not rooted in unpleasant experiences of the past.

Naive investors will develop an aversion to a particular sector, instrument or asset class after they burn their fingers in the market. Dvesha is the opposite of Raga or attachment. Aversion arises towards things that produce unpleasant experiences. Aversion towards equity may be the result of

1. relying on hearsay
2. selling the winners early and holding on to losers
3. Trying to time the volatile equity market

Relying on hearsay

Hearsay is probably the biggest reason for low domestic retail participation in equities. One hears people describing the equity market as a gambling den. Often, people who have little or zero experience with the equity market declare with authority that investing in equity is a sure way to lose money.

Hearsay also lures investors into the market without arming them with knowledge. It is good old Avidya at play. If one invests while one's mind is steeped in Avidya, one comes to sorrow. Often, unscrupulous advisers tempt unsuspecting people with stories of fantastic gains within unrealistically short time frames. Alternatively, someone they trust advises them or they are in awe of a friend or associate who has made it big in the equity market. Generally, investors who claim to have made fast money share partial information with new investors. These 'successful' investors conveniently share just their successful investment stories; they seldom share their bad experiences as they want to be seen as rational creatures who make the best of decisions. Those who take such advice at face value often bruise themselves badly. Being their first or second investment, this type of experience lasts for a long time. Often, they live the remainder of their lives in mortal fear of the equity market. Once bitten twice shy.

Selling winners early and holding on to losers

Most investors sell profit making stocks too early without waiting for the stock price to realize its full potential whereas they hold on too long to the stocks that have depreciated in price. It is Dvesha towards loss making stocks which makes investors defer the feeling of unpleasantness. On the other hand, investors are more likely to sell a winning position too soon as it allows them to enjoy the feeling of winning faster. This tendency harms the overall investment returns of the investors.

Trying to time the volatile equity market

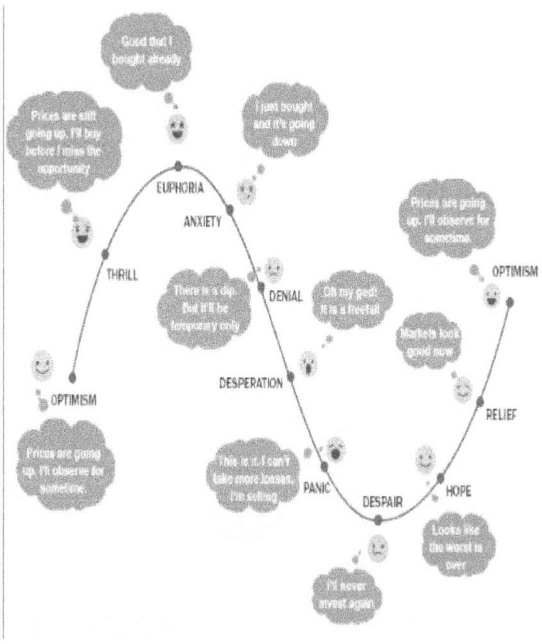

The equity market inspires cycles of emotions. A bull-market (when share prices are rising) fires the market with optimism and thrill. A bear market (when share prices are falling) drives people into despair.

New investors lose money not because the markets are bad, but because they are defeated by their attempts to time the markets on the advice of ignorant or unscrupulous advisers. One should instead focus on buying quality stocks when the market is at its low point. It is best to stay invested for a period of time, till valuations of the stock rise to justify its intrinsic value. Please keep in mind that time in the market is more important than timing the market. This simple Yoga investment Mantra helps one deal with Dvesha.

Equity markets are volatile and uncertain by nature. Not all the factors that shape the performance of a particular stock or the market as a whole can be predicted.

Is volatility a good thing or bad?

Well, if volatility is here to stay, one better be friends with it. If we take a look at the recent past, there were events (unknowns) like Brexit, surgical strikes, the outcome of the US Presidential elections or the demonetisation exercise, threats from N. Korea, talks of trade wars between US and China, etc. Being extraneous in nature, these events would have little or no impact on the Indian economy, but the markets reacted sharply to such events. What we saw was impatient investors selling off their positions and booking big losses. This is the mentality of the herd. In such a situation, what a smart investor really does is perceives the fall as an opportunity to buy quality stocks at a discount. One should research for oneself and decide. Volatility should be perceived as a source of opportunity for the Yoga investor.

While the market appears volatile and cyclical in nature in the short run, the graph for the long run reveals an upward trajectory. A short or medium term investor often finds it difficult to earn returns in the down-cycle of the markets. In order to earn decent returns, one has to participate in the market up-cycle and remain invested till the near end of the cycle to earn handsome returns. But this is easier said than done, as it is difficult to gauge the start or the end of the cycle, given the high degree of uncertainty that marks the equity market. However, in the long term, the equity markets have given best returns across all asset classes. One needs to be both patient (by investing long term) and smart (by buying on dips) to be able to create wealth.

Keeping Dvesha at bay

If one does not have the time or knowledge to monitor the day to day happenings of the market, one can opt for staggered investments in the form of a Systematic Investment Plan (SIP) in equity mutual funds or a basket of stocks.

SIP involves investing a fixed amount, big or small, at regular intervals (say monthly) in the equity markets, irrespective of the price of the stock purchased. Investing regularly in small amounts is not only convenient, it also helps investors ride the market ups and downs and make volatility their friend. Here are a few advantages of investing by the SIP route:

1. **Easy on the wallet:** Ideal for small investors as it involves a small amount to be set aside monthly.
2. **Discipline:** It inculcates the habit of regular saving.
3. **Reduces Volatility:** Since one invests regularly over a long period of time, it neutralises the effect of market ups and downs and eliminates the need to time the market.
4. **Rupee Cost Averaging:** It averages the cost across market cycles and, therefore, reduces one's overall cost of purchase.
5. **Diversification:** SIP helps one create a diversified portfolio of stocks over a period of time with very small regular commitments.

Having started an SIP, most people either stop it or withdraw the corpus in a bear phase of the market. It is extremely important that for the SIP to bear fruit one must stay invested over a long period across market cycles.

सतुदीर्घकालनैरन्तर्यसत्काराअदराअसेवितोदृढभूमिः ॥

Sa tu dirgha kala nairantarya satkara sevito drudha bhumihi

Three conditions must be fulfilled in order for a practice to be firmly established:

1. must continue for a long time
2. there should be no interruptions
3. must be pursued with devotion and in a spirit of reverence

– 1.14 Patanjali Yoga Sutra

Similarly, systematic investment automated over a long period of time, without interruptions, helps combat the loss aversion feeling and creates wealth in the long run. If one is not involved in the intimate details of each purchase and sale of a stock, one is less likely to feel so psychologically tied to a particular decision.

Conclusion

Primarily, there are 3 reasons for Dvesha, i.e. hearsay, holding on to losing stocks and trying to time the volatile market. The Klesha of hearsay and holding on to losing stocks can be minimized if one seeks professional expertise through Mutual Funds or invests with target / stop-losses defined by research experts from reputed brokerage firms. The Yoga Mantras to stay away from trying to time the market are 'Practice SIP' and 'Buy on dips'. These are the two most effective ways to beat volatility and avoid unpleasant experiences. Having learned the lesson, one should try not to develop a deep aversion towards equity investments. In other words, one must experience cycles of super-normal returns, normal returns, no returns and negative returns for one to be able to earn long term positive returns. If the initial experiences were bad, one should take it as the tuition fee paid towards learning, and continue investing. Stopping after falling down or after incurring a loss deprives one of potential profits that can be earned if one remains invested in equities for long periods.

Chapter 5

Abhinivesha

ABHINIVESHA: FEAR OF LOSS

स्वरसवाहीविदुषोऽपितथारूढोभिनिवेशः ॥

Swarasavahia vidishopi tatharudo abhinivesah

Flowing on its own nature, Love of life exists even in the wise

– 2.9 Patanjali Yoga Sutra

The Sutra quoted above says that even the wise experience fear and it makes them act carefully. This fear of losing everything that is intrinsic to all beings in the state of Avidya, has been described as Abhinivesha in the Yoga Sutra.

Abhinivesh or fear of death is the outcome of the first four Kleshas, namely Avidya, Asmita, Raga and Dvesha. One who is in Avidya (ignorance) is bound to suffer from a misplaced sense of self or Asmita (ego). The one who experiences Asmita makes choices on the basis of Raga (attachment) and Dvesha (aversion). Attachment and aversion are based on pleasant and unpleasant memories, respectively. One experiences aversion to that which brought pain in the past. One experiences attachment to anything that brought pleasure in the past. Therefore, ignorance results in a deluded sense of self-worth in an investor, who acts out of irrational likes and dislikes and fears a loss of money. To be a Yogi is to step out of this stream of memory and act neither under the influence of Raga or Dvesha but to exercise Viveka (differentiating right from wrong) on the basis of Vidya (knowledge).

However, with the awakening of Viveka, as one acquires Vidya (knowledge of the market), one gradually starts freeing oneself from the clutches of Avidya, which is the greatest cause for sorrow.

In the world of investing, the Abhinivesh can be of three kinds

1. Fear of loss of capital
2. Fear of change within
3. Fear of change in markets.

Let us explore these fears in greater detail -

1. Fear of Loss:

The fear of loss is a major barrier to healthy investing. Fear of loss may prevent one from recognizing opportunities for creating wealth. If one tells an investor that their Rs. 1,00,000 invested has grown to Rs. 1,10,000 in a year, they may not be very happy. But if one tells them that their investment of Rs. 1,00,000 has now become Rs. 90,000, it may upset them sorely. This phenomenon has been called 'loss aversion' by behavioural finance experts who study how human psychology affects investment behaviour. Loss aversion makes humans hate losing more than they enjoy gaining. Losses have more emotional impact than an equivalent gain.

Abhinivesha or fear of loss has its origin in one of the following two causes.

a. **Personal Experience:** It is possible to develop cold feet when considering equity if one has suffered erosion in one's investment value during the last market correction, say post the Lehman crisis in 2008 or the dotcom burst in 2000. The value of one's investment may have declined by 50–55% over a short span of time with no opportunity to react.

b. **Experiences of family or friends:** Abhinivesha may be rooted in memories of losses suffered by immediate family members or friends. It is also possible that the fear of loss is rooted in the advice tendered by people who lost their hard earned savings in the market. Such 'experienced' well-wishers may advise one to beware of the equity

market and choose safety over rewards when it comes to investment.

Fear of loss may prevent one from recognising opportunities for creating wealth. Most investors park their investments in fixed income assets that give them predictable and assured low returns. The fact that only 16–17% of the Indian domestic population is invested in equity markets, in spite of superior returns, is largely an effect of this Klesha.

Abhinivesha (*fear of loss*) makes an investor risk averse as they are reluctant to choose an investment with an unpredictable rate of return over one with a lower but certain rate of return. This fear of loss prevents an investor from participating in investments that are volatile in nature like equities but have the potential to offer higher returns to compensate for the risk undertaken.

2. Fear of change within:

Investors cling to their ego which manifests in thoughts like 'my investment', 'my sector', 'my price', or 'my investment style'. Therefore, they fear they would lose something if they acted any differently from the way they have always done. It is important that investments are viewed independently in the current context without any bias or prejudice to a pet theory.

Many times investors have been found to cling to their pet theories, say due to their previous experience where they were rewarded whether on the back of their concerted efforts or their good fortune. Investors that made a fortune in the sugar sector in the 2008–2010 phase tried to find bargains later, despite fundamental changes in the demand-supply equation of the sector. Such investors fail to read the changes in dynamics due to Kleshas like

Avidya (due to their failure to understand changed fundamentals), Asmita (failure to accept that they have made a mistake in taking exposure due to their half baked knowledge) and Raga (attachment to a specific sector because of its past performance). They keep holding the investment without realising the loss of opportunity of recovering their losses by investing in a better sector with improved fundamentals.

3. Fear of change in markets:

Markets are volatile by nature and have never given linear returns. This seemingly zigzag movement of markets in a short term makes people jittery and amplifies the Abhinivesha within. Abhinivesha strongly grips the minds of investors during bear phases in equity markets. The retail market participation evaporates and ill informed investors shun the equity market. However, these times are historically the best phases to invest in. Let us explain this with the help of historical return data of the Sensex performance over the last few decades. The graph below depicts the returns the Sensex offered, post a downfall in the markets. The returns are calculated over 1 year from the lows of the year in which the market crashed.

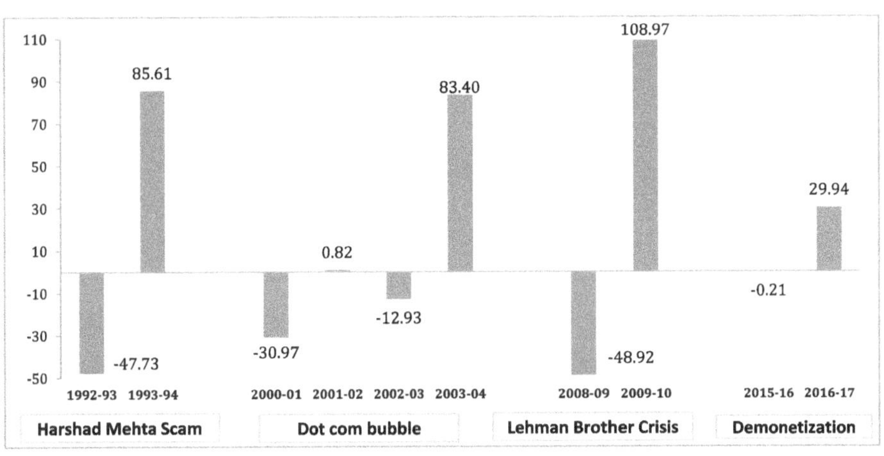

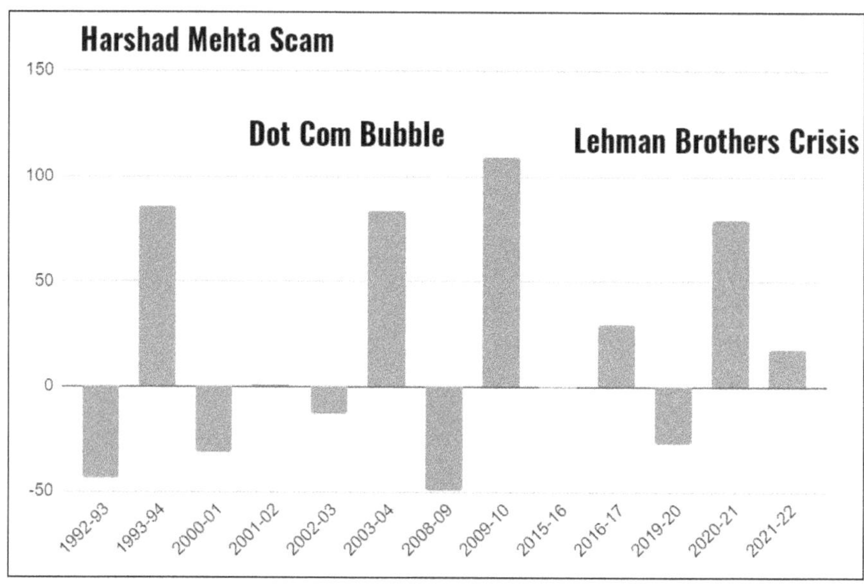

The data above shows how the markets have bounced back and investors who had invested in the darkest hour of the market have been rewarded handsomely for their undaunted spirit and presence of mind. In the event of a market crash, investors should gather their nerves and instead of getting bogged down by the Abhinivesh or pessimism around, invest or at least stay rooted in the Vidya that every dip is a buying opportunity.

Yoga explains through a concept named "Anitya bhavna" (A-Nitya-meaning no continuity) that the world is a place of impermanence and the stock market is no exception. Let us delve deeper.

Anitya bhavna

'What was in the morning is not at midday; what was at midday is not at night,'- for all things are transitory or Anitya. If one is disturbed or unhappy about things life is throwing at them, it helps to step back from problems and consider the bigger picture. When everything seems to be against one, they need to observe

what the truth is and internalize the thought that this phase is not permanent. Similarly, in the short run, market participants may feel that the market is against the investor's expectations and all their investments are going wrong. However, in the long-run, investments made in a portfolio of stocks with strong fundamentals do consistently yield handsome returns. One should therefore not get overly worked up if a stock with strong fundamentals fares badly in the short run. If due diligence has been done on a stock and one has arrived at the conclusion that a stock's fundamentals are strong, it will always catch up in the long run. However, it is also true that there are times when the best of calculations go awry. In such situations, Anitya Bhavna prepares one for the turmoil that is part and parcel of life; Anitya Bhavna prepares one for all eventualities. In all such situations, if one has adopted the feeling of Anitya Bhavna, one will not obsess about what life has thrown at them. One focuses on what best can be done under the given circumstances. The art of living is, after all, the art of responding well.

Often, things are not as bad as they are painted to be.

The news industry thrives on sensationalism because a sensational, juicy rumour is more palatable than straightforward accurate news to an audience with an extremely short attention span. All humans have a tendency to believe hearsay and some enjoy gossip. All this noise clouds the judgment of new investors and pushes them to decisions that are rash. Best way to escape this is to not think too much about the possible negative impacts that every new information will cause on one's investments. One may soon realise that things are really not as bad as they are being made to seem. The attitude 'this too shall pass' is an important one for anyone who ventures into the market.

Keeping Abhinivesha at bay

Here are a few Yoga Mantras on overcoming the fear of loss, fear of change within and fear of change in markets -

1. Avoiding investment in equities means one is losing money anyway! To minimize the fear of loss, one must understand that the purchasing power of one's savings will be worth less next year than it is this year, and even lesser the year after that. This, in economic terms, is called inflation.

If one is saving their money in fixed income products like Bank FDs or MF Debt schemes, they are getting about 2–3% inflation adjusted returns. This is not enough to keep pace with inflation and taxes.

Above return data calculated from 1979 till 2018; avg. inflation assumed at 8.1%

Therefore, it should be clear by now that one cannot ignore equity as an asset class and must find ways to participate in it more effectively, either through well researched stocks validated by experts or by leaving investments at the hands of professional mutual fund managers.

2. Change is the only constant: To minimize the fear of change within, one must acknowledge that 'The only constant in life is change'. One should avoid getting espoused to a concept; one should always test the validity by questioning its relevance. One has to be mindful that one is not getting biased by the constrained thought process and should be on a constant lookout for knowledge of new developments that would challenge the basic fundamentals on which the premises of investments were built up. Strictly avoid complacency! Do not fear accepting that one has a lack of knowledge. Admit that nobody is born intelligent, everyone gets educated sometime or the other. As they say, *"It's human to err, to persist in error (out of pride) is diabolical (disgracefully bad)."* And finally, avoid unnecessary attachment. One invests to grow one's net worth, not to prove their superiority over others. If the investment rationale changes, accept it and exit before making further losses or losing out on other opportunities which may not only help recover the losses but give higher returns.

3. Be greedy when others are fearful - To minimize the fear of market volatility or downturns, one must explore whether the value of a fundamentally strong stock has come down due to prevailing bearish sentiments in the market or otherwise. This approach helps one view the bear phase as a buying opportunity, which enables one to increase one's holdings of a specific stock in one's portfolio. A value-cum-growth investor realises that if the fundamentals of the company are intact and growth is visible, it is just a matter of time before the market will factor the performance of the company into the share price.

For example, the recent Covid Crisis brought much ambiguity in the market, same as the levels of 2008 Global Financial Crisis. The Russia-Saudi Arabia war added fuel to the fire with oil prices falling to surprisingly low levels. With businesses closing down and people left with no choice but to lock themselves in their homes, the Indian stock market collapsed drastically. However, investors who adopted the 'buy on dip' strategy, and were determined to ride out the market's intermittent volatility with patience managed to earn good returns.

Moreover, investors should understand that extraneous events, which have resulted in the equity market correction, have a direct bearing on just a few sectors. They should wait for the prices of particular stocks to drop below their intrinsic valuation so that they can buy. The intrinsic value, as explained by Benjamin Graham, is defined as the value of the security based on its assets, earnings, dividends, definite prospects, etc., and justified by them. It may or may not be different from the current market value of the security. At this point, taking a contrarian bet, a value-cum-growth investor can enter the market to buy stocks in sectors that have not been affected by the event but had their market price beaten down simply because the entire market fell.

Conclusion

When fear grips the mind, we can switch our mind to focus on just the opposite by the 'power of positive thinking'. A concept in Yoga, which reinforces the above thought, is known as Pratipaksha Bhavana.

Pratipaksha Bhavna

वितर्कबाधनेप्रतिप्रक्षभावनम्

Vitarka-bādhane pratiprakṣa-bhāvanam

When disturbed by negative thoughts, opposite (positive) ones should be thought of. This is pratipaksha bhavana.

– 2.33 Patanjali **Yoga Sutra**

Pratipaksha Bhavana is the attitude of cultivating and holding on to an attitude that is diametrically opposed to the one that is holding us at a lower level. Pratipaksha Bhavana literally means 'moving to the other side of the mansion' which implies moving from negative thoughts to positive ones. Instead of spiralling down a staircase of negative thoughts, one must try to seize and overcome these thoughts at the very first step. Yogis who practice Pratipaksha

Bhavana will use the awareness that they are getting provoked by something or someone and train their mind to look at it as a test of their patience. By seeing the same facts in a new light, they will ensure that their mind is not unduly disturbed.

Pratipaksha Bhavana calls for letting go and erasing the pessimism within us and replacing it with optimism. We all know that occurrence of certain negative scenarios is inevitable as both the negative and positive are part and parcel of life. We must not judge ourselves for having those thoughts, and should instead refrain from clinging on to them. It is in our hands to not be perturbed by these instances and shift our focus towards positive memories with ease and gentleness.

Similarly, in the equity markets, when one develops fear of loss or fear of change in oneself or fear of market volatility, one must remind oneself that fundamentally sound stocks prevail in the long run and always bounce back after a sharp fall, rewarding investors handsomely. Successful investors are those who take a contrarian approach and keep investing despite lots of fear and negativity surrounding the markets.

Remember - everything one wants is on the other side of fear!

Module 2

Bhavas of Investing

Preface

The word 'Bhava' stands for an expression of feeling or attitude. In Yoga, the term Bhavna is used in the context of a conscious expression of four distinct mental tendencies. The practices of Yoga Asanas (postural training) are associated with four major important groups of or feelings. *Asana* is not just an external form. In the performance of the *Asana* there is a lot of Bhavna or feeling that is also included. The right state of feelings, attention, attitude, state of mind, relaxation in the muscles, etc. will eventually lead to perfection of the Asanas. The regular and repeated practice of Yoga techniques with the correct accompanying 'Bhava' slowly augments subtle and gross energies. An investor whose thinking does not strengthen the Bhavas is likely to succumb to the pressures that come with the volatility inherent in the equity market. Yoga considers the intellect or *Buddhi* of paramount importance in a human being as it is that which directs all actions. *Buddhi* expresses itself through four prominent Bhavas:

1. Dharma (duty),
2. Gyana (knowledge),
3. Vairagya (detachment) and
4. Aishwarya (achievement)

Dharma

Contrary to common belief, Dharma means duty or righteousness and not religion. At every point in life, one needs to ask oneself what one's righteous duty in that given situation is. Dharma is an expression of one's intellect. It ensures that we do that which is ethically right.

It is said that the one who walks the path of Dharma is saved from pain and suffering. In fact, Yoga philosophy outlines a hierarchy of

duties like a) duty towards oneself b) duty towards family c) duty towards work and d) duty towards society or nation.

Neglecting this hierarchy of self-family-work-society is a sure recipe for disaster. Those who over-work to provide for their families by missing their meals end up harming their health. Similarly, somebody who does not create provisions for retirement, insurance, child's education, etc., ends up harming themself financially. It is only the strong, the capable and the competent who can serve. As a part of duty towards one's family, investors have to ensure adequate funds for their children's education, a roof above their head and financial security for themselves and their spouse, post retirement. They should ensure that they make adequate provisions for themselves and their family before they decide to do their Dharma to society and to the world.

Gyana

Gyana refers to the habit of understanding things and gaining knowledge about any situation before taking action. A Yogi in Gyana Bhavna has a spirit of open curiosity towards life. It is the spirit, which, propelled by curiosity, pushes one to question, understand, analyse and experience. One who exudes the Bhavna of Gyana constantly acquires knowledge and acts out of that knowledge. The internet age offers huge opportunities for Vidya (learning) but it is only that which is grasped in the form of understanding (Gyana) that can actually help. Applied to investment, what this means is that the best of market research is of no use to one who does not have the capacity to grasp the knowledge as Gyana. One who expresses the Bhavna of Gyana shows a remarkable ability to use existing knowledge to a specific situation.

Vairagya

Excessive emotional attachment to one's wealth tells on one's mental wellbeing and health in the long run. We should learn to be objective in life. We should keep a little distance from any given situation and learn to have a 'witness-like attitude'. We should learn to surrender to a higher reality and learn to keep our ego aside. After all, the outcome of an investment in a particular stock or mutual fund scheme is not affected in any manner by our expectations from it. It is therefore imperative that after due diligence has been done on an investment, we let go emotionally and stop worrying excessively about the outcome.

While Raga refers to attachment, Vairagya is an attitude of indifference to attachment or Raga. It is the capacity of the investor to step back from an object one is attached or attracted to and view it dispassionately. Vairagya makes one objective, and keeps one from taking emotional decisions. Householders with Vairagya Bhavna take care of their family dutifully. They do not, however, get emotionally disturbed by the inevitable drama involved in being a family person. Such a state has been described as one of 'being in the world but not of the world'.

Aishwarya

Before one achieves success, one has to acknowledge within oneself that success is possible. Aishwarya Bhavna is an expression or attitude of quiet poise that communicates achievement, satisfaction and knowledge along with extreme humility. It is the culmination of the Dharma, Gyana and Vairagya Bhavas. A Yogi or Yogic investor who manifests Aishwarya Bhavna exudes strength, will power, self-reliance, forbearance and fortitude. For him whose

Buddhi or intellect radiates or expresses Aishwarya, wealth comes easily.

To summarise, what is required to begin with is a portfolio that takes care of duty towards self, family and society (Dharma). One also needs a mind that grasps the importance of knowledge gained through research (Gyana) and a readiness to do what is required without getting affected by the Drama in the market (Vairagya). A person who follows these steps comes to a place of certainty within (Aishwarya) that attracts great wealth.

By understanding these potentialities of the intellect, one can consciously work towards developing them within oneself through the discipline of Yoga. Yoga provides us with the practical tools to develop the Buddhi's potentialities for these Bhavas.

BHAVA PURUSHA: A representation of the hierarchy of Dharma, Gyana, Vairagya and Aishwarya. The roots are Dharma, water and sunlight are Gyana, patience is Vairagya and the flower and fruits are Aishwarya.

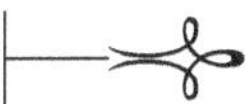

Chapter 1

Dharma

DHARMA

The Yoga Sutra outlines four Dharmas that are incumbent upon an individual: Duty to oneself, duty to family, duty towards one's work and duty to society. The foremost thing to remember about Dharma is that the investor has to have a step-wise approach, without neglecting the hierarchy of Dharma outlined in Yoga. Dharma Bhava represents 'Self direction'; it also embodies the philosophy of 'External control leads to internal control and self mastery'. Meditative postures, like Sukhasanam, describe the Bhava of Dharma.

These Yoga Asanas help one change from Adharma (negative bhava) to Dharma (positive Bhava); these Asanas inculcate discipline, build up a healthy relationship with one's own Self thereby bringing about peace and quietness to the practitioner. Constant practice of these Asanas helps build strength of fearless, positive conviction about the self.

This four-fold categorisation has important implications for the Yoga investor.

Dharma towards oneself

The standard flight safety announcement in a passenger aircraft warns travellers that 'in the event of a sudden loss of cabin pressure, oxygen masks will automatically descend from the ceiling. Grab the mask, and pull it over your face. Please secure your mask first before assisting others'. The instructions are rooted in clarity because in practice, it is only those who operate from a place of security and safety in a crisis who can extend help to others. Neglecting this hierarchy leads to several problems at the intra and inter-personal level. It is only the healthy and wealthy who can undertake their duties towards their family, their work and society at large. A penniless person who advices others on investment strategy has no moral standing. Charity, in other words, does *not* begin at home but begins with one's own self.

Most people devote little time to growing their wealth. We work hard to earn our salaries but are lazy to the point of being careless towards investing wisely with the aim of increasing our wealth.

This state of non-worrying can only come to those who have 'made enough money' over a period of time. Such a state comes to those with a sound financial plan early in life. It has to be a plan that

involves regular targeted savings with rational asset allocation and disciplined long-term investments. These are people who have been mindful in performing their Dharma to themselves.

I. Plan for contingency

Life may not always go as planned but preparing for various possible life events can help one manage them better, financially. To meet uncertain events like a loss of job or medical emergency, one must build up a contingency fund, which should be separate from investments for anticipated events, like marriage or retirement. To build a contingency fund, one can give an auto-instruction to direct a certain sum from their salary account every month to a recurring deposit, which will lock in their money for a fixed time frame. One can also invest in instruments such as short-term debt funds or liquid funds to earn higher returns without compromising on liquidity. Health and life insurance should also be a part of one's financial plans. A term policy for life cover and mediclaim policy for health should also be incorporated into the portfolio.

II. Plan debt

While it is ideal to refrain from loan products, as they restrict one's financial freedom, it may not always be possible. In case one needs to avail a loan, one should always go in for a term loan and try to get rid of it at the earliest. One should try not to delay payment of loan installments as late payment fees may trap them in a vicious circle of ballooning debt. The same is applicable to credit card transactions. High-interest on loan installments and credit card transactions can create a debt trap where individuals, at times, apply for top-ups or fresh loans to repay the existing ones. One can set up calendar alerts to ensure that one does not miss the due dates. While prioritizing loan repayments, one should start by paying off the highest interest loans (usually credit card outstandings and loans), and then work one's way down to the lower interest ones.

III. Plan the tax outgo

Keeping tax outgo at the minimum is an important part of one's Dharma to oneself. Equity Linked Saving Schemes (ELSS) offered by mutual fund houses are an important part of prudent tax planning. An informed approach to tax management minimises the drain of earnings and makes more funds available for wealth creation. Because of their exposure to the equity market, ELSS funds help one earn inflation-beating returns over the long-term.

However, tax planning should go beyond annual tax saving investments to protect one from losing money on heads like capital gains and wealth tax.

For instance, if an investor parks Rs. 10 Lakh for some long term goal in a government bond (fixed income) offering an 8% rate of interest for a 10–15 year period, while the risks are limited, the returns hardly beat the rate of inflation, and the capital gains from the investment would be taxable. A tax efficient strategy would be to put the same money in the equity market either directly in fundamentally strong stocks or via index ETFs or Equity oriented Mutual Fund schemes. One can continue to withdraw money to the tune of 8.8% after every year. Withdrawing 8.8% from the corpus every year would offer the post tax returns of 8% (accounting for 10% capital gains tax). Further, the records of the equity markets to deliver superior returns are widely understood to have improved, following economic reforms in the country. These facts make a strong case for investing in the equity markets either directly or through various equity-linked instruments for tenures ranging from

10 to 15 years, as stated in this example, as the possibility of returns are considerably higher.

Dharma towards family

After individuals have fulfilled their Dharma towards themself, they are required to fulfill their Dharma towards the members of their family. Dharma towards the family includes caring for the financial well being of one's loved ones by ensuring their needs are adequately met. This includes addressing their present needs as well as planning for their future. Such goal-based planning should begin early in life and include goals like buying a house, education/ marriage of children, travelling abroad, and retirement. Such a plan has to incorporate elements like targeted and regular savings, proper asset allocation and disciplined long term investments.

Sound Financial Planning

Financial planning is the art of making monetary arrangements for achieving clearly outlined goals. A thorough analysis of one's current financial health is the first step towards creating a sound financial plan. How much does one own? How much does one owe? What are one's monthly outgoings? Does one have any/adequate insurance cover? After the current situation has been assessed, and goals have been set, one has to decide on an asset allocation strategy to reach one's goals and start investing as per plan. It is necessary to keep a track of the performance of one's investments to check if everything is going according to plan and take detours or make changes if required.

One may draw one's financial plan on one's own or engage the services of a professional financial adviser, preferably backed by a reputed institution with a proven success ratio.

The credibility of an adviser should be submitted to a careful background check before any advice is accepted; one may, of course, draw their own financial plan if one is financially literate. Either way, a good plan is a must for all who wish to protect their families and their wealth from volatility. Such a plan paves the path for long-term gains and gives one the wisdom to endure short-term pains.

Sound financial planning calls for the following steps:

Step 1: Determine the current financial situation

The health of one's current finances can be gauged on the basis of one's income, savings, living expenses and debts. Listing the current asset and debt balances along with other heads of expenditure to arrive at a clear picture of current finances will provide one with a basic foundation for financial planning.

The accuracy of information on one's financial health and the competence of one's financial advisor are the two pillars on which the success of one's financial planning rests. An adviser carries out a thorough due-diligence of one's financial health on the basis of the following information:

- Assets and liabilities
- Income and expenditure
- Risk attitude, tolerance and capacity

Step 2: Develop financial goals

Investors must think of the life that lies ahead for them and their family; how do they want it to shape out? It is important at this stage to differentiate one's needs from one's wants. One may desire a fancy luxury car and there is nothing wrong with it but before that

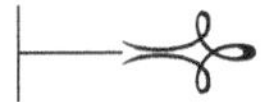

they must fulfill their family's needs like building a fund for their child's education, a retirement corpus, and an emergency kitty.

It is of vital importance to be clear about one's financial goals. Others may suggest financial goals for one; however, it is for one to decide which goals to pursue. It is important that one asks oneself simple questions like:

- What are the foreseen milestones of my life?
- When do I wish to accomplish this particular goal? In 5 years, 10 years, 20 years or 30 years?
- Are my goals quantifiable and achievable?
- Am I willing to accept a high market risk to achieve my investment goals or would a conservative portfolio serve me better?
- Also, realistically how close am I to my goals?
- Are my saving levels sufficient to meet these goals?
- Do I have adequate life insurance cover, in case something happens to me?
- Do I have a will?

Although, one may already be aware of this information, it is wise to write down one's goals in order to gain a clear picture of one's overall financial situation. This helps them as well as their financial advisor who ends up in a better situation to offer prudent advice.

Step 3: Analyse the data

Once one has gathered data on one's financial health and set goals, the information at hand has to be subjected to intense analysis. Let's say an investor's retirement planning goal assumes a retirement age that is 30 years away, and they expect the Rs. 500,000 they have already saved for this purpose to yield them a 12% return on their

investments. They further expect to save Rs. 10,000 per month, going forward. Given these numbers, at the end of 30 years, they will roughly end up with Rs. 5 Cr.

Such calculations are a necessary part of one's data analysis.

If one doesn't have a financial calculator, one can use online help. One can plug in the numbers and calculate if the retirement kitty is enough to fulfill the needs that must be met in the winter years of one's life. By factoring inflation and the rising cost of healthcare into one's estimates, one can make them more realistic. Is this figure enough? Are one's retirement goals achievable? Often, the initial estimates are not adequate to reach the goals one sets out to achieve and the plan calls for some tweaking.

Developing alternatives is crucial for making good decisions. Although many factors influence the available alternatives, possible courses of action usually fall into these categories:

- Continue on the same course of action
- Expand the current situation
- Change the current situation
- Take a new course of action

Continuing with the previous example, if the investor needs Rs. 7 Cr for retirement, instead of the Rs. 5 Cr arrived at earlier, strategies will have to be worked out to step up the monthly investments or increase the allocation to an asset class, like equity, that promises to deliver better returns.

The process of investment decision-making calls for creativity and out-of-the-box thinking along with a careful consideration of all possible alternatives at hand.

Step 4: Create and implement a financial action plan

Once the data at hand has been analysed and the contours of the strategy outlined, one has to create an action plan and stick to it. With the passage of time, as one investment milestone is crossed, another comes into focus.

It is not enough to draw a plan. One has to summon the discipline to put it into action. Saving Rs. 10,000 or Rs. 20,000 per month may prove to be more difficult in reality than it is on paper. Successful investors say that just getting started is an important part of attaining success in the wealth creation process. One doesn't need to start out at a high level of savings or at an advanced level of investment strategy. One could learn to invest with just one fund or start saving small amounts every week to build up one's first investment.

An investment broker can smoothen the process for an investor by helping them purchase stocks, bonds, mutual funds and insurance.

If one is new to investing or financial planning, it makes sense to go with low-risk, conservative strategies even if the returns are not as high as one desires. Once an investor is comfortable with the strategy and accustomed to the low returns, one may calibrate the strategy to accommodate higher risk and commensurate higher returns. Jumping into an investment situation without testing waters may prove to be more challenging than one thinks. If, for instance, one is a new investor in equities, it may be better for one to invest in a mix of equity-based mutual funds or begin one's equity SIPs with an Index ETF before investing actively in stocks.

Once one gets comfortable with equity-linked instruments, one can either research stocks on one's own or rely on expert research or seek a broker's advice on investing in stocks directly.

Correct assessment and implementation of one's financial action plan are the most important steps in one's financial planning journey so that one's hard earned money grows according to expectations.

Step 5: Monitoring and taking corrective action

Financial planning is a dynamic process that does not end when one takes a particular action. Market realities shift every moment and plans have to evolve to respond to the changed situation. Monitoring the shifts in the investment ecosystem and tweaking the investment plan from time to time are a part of the game. Events such as marriage, the birth of children, career changes impact one's financial health. There are also financial changes beyond our control, like changes in tax laws, interest rates, inflation, equity market fluctuations and economic recession.

In the light of the above factors, reviewing one's financial plans becomes necessary. Let's take a look at the reasons for subjecting one's financial plan to periodic review:

Goal versus achievement: By the time one's investment grows to the Rs. 1 Cr that is needed to buy a house in the neighbourhood of one's choice, one may realise that the market price has moved significantly higher than anticipated. It may also happen that one has not progressed or moved towards a particular financial goal since the plan was created. It becomes imperative, in such situations, to review one's investments and revise one's asset allocation, if required. In such cases, it may also be prudent to push a goal further away, if possible, or relook at alternatives. A review of one's financial plan enables one to determine whether the predetermined goals are achievable, given the present circumstances. It also allows one to make them more realistic.

Change in income: One may have received a hike in salary recently or may be close to receiving it soon. A big change in income would directly impact financial plans. It may not only lead to the early maturity of one's goals but also prompt one to dream bigger in life. Similarly, any unfortunate event, like a pay-cut, may have an adverse impact on one's financial status and therefore call for re-evaluation and revision of the financial plan.

Contingencies and expenses: Medical emergencies may burn a big hole in one's monthly savings, especially if no provisions have been made in their financial plan for such contingencies. The number of accidents and medical costs associated with them are continually rising. Even if one claims medical insurance to meet these expenses, the subsequent premiums that one pays for insurance cover may be higher.

Number of dependents: Change in marital status, birth of a child or the death of a loved one can largely impact cash flows and consequently affect one's financial plan. For example, if one's family is growing, the life insurance cover will have to be raised, so that the financial requirements of the dependents are covered even in one's absence. However, if one's children are grown up adults and are no longer financially dependent on them, then they need to reconsider their insurance portfolio as well, and take a greater coverage in health insurance while also resetting life priorities. It is also important to write a will and select nominees for one's assets in order to avoid any disputes after their death.

Change in tax status: Changes in income tax laws or one's income may push one into a new tax bracket, which affects cash flows either negatively or positively and, by extension, affects one's financial plans. In case the change places a higher tax burden on one, it calls for a revision of their financial plan to reduce the tax liability.

New goals: Priorities change over a period of time. For example, when one is in their early 20s, one's priorities would include going for a holiday twice a year and spending heavily on lifestyle. But one's spending habits and goals change once they have kids and have a family to support. Similarly, one might have new goals and other added responsibilities apart from existing ones, which may not be accounted for in their old financial plan. New strategies and investments might have to be incorporated in the plan to meet these new objectives.

Change in risk appetite: For example, if one is a young investor or is financially secure (one has children that are well-placed in life), they would be willing to take more risk. Hence their portfolio would be skewed towards high risk-high return asset classes, like equities or real estate. But if one finds themselves facing a situation of early or untimely retirement, their risk tolerance level is likely to be lower, which would then reflect in the asset allocation in their plan. Similarly, if one is close to realisation of a certain goal, the asset mix for that goal can be shifted to a less volatile asset class, such as debt and other fixed income instruments, as the relatively high risk in the original allocation need not be borne in the face of the changed situation. During the COVID crisis starting 2019, there was a drastic shift in the risk appetite of investors. While lower markets were a huge opportunity to buy stocks at a cheaper price, there was a significant increase in healthcare expenditure in homes. The whole environment was fearful, which led to many investors being risk averse, or not investing in the market at all.

While monitoring and course correction is considered to be the last step in financial planning, in essence, it is a constant process

through the life of the investment. Step 5 involves the review of all previously laid out steps, right from reassessing one's current financial situation to setting out newer or modified goals, to analysing data and formulating an altered financial action plan, if need be. Life changes, laws change and so does one's plan. That is probably why the process or subject has not been called creating a financial plan - it's called financial planning!

A rupee saved is a rupee earned. So, while goal-based financial planning helps one's money grow, a tax efficient strategy helps them save their hard earned rupee. A tax efficient strategy includes tax-saving instruments, like Public Provident Fund, as the interest earned on them is tax-free and the entire balance can be withdrawn on maturity. Similarly, there are provisions for claiming tax savings on expenditure made on children's education, like annual fees, education loans, etc. In addition, the investments made in Mediclaim policies for a family including children and parents are also exempt from taxes.

Also, it is one's Dharma to impart financial education to members of one's family, including children and spouse. One must impress upon one's loved ones the virtues of becoming cost conscious and the value of investing as a habit. Even at a tender age, kids can be made to learn the value of a rupee and encouraged to save for their goals. A child can be given an investing account or app and can be encouraged to start saving regularly, no matter how small the initial investment. Financial education is the need of the hour. It should be taught to children in primary school and not just to students pursuing higher education in particular streams like commerce. A vast majority of the educated Indian population parks their hard earned money in fixed income instruments, real-estate or gold. It is the Dharma of each one among us to urge, and inspire others to have a proper investment plan and highlight the benefits of investing a significant portion of equity in the long-term. It is not just important to create wealth for the family but to involve them in the process so that they can take care of their finances and plan for their future, thereby resulting in wealth creation for all.

Dharma towards work

Work is considered a part of worship in the Indian tradition. We spend at least one-third of our day at our workplace, which gives us our daily bread. Money, i.e. a salary or business/professional income, comes from fulfilling our Dharma towards work. The Bhagavad Gita says, "Karmanay vadikaaraste ma faleshu kadachana," which translates into 'Work without any expectation of results'. When at the workplace, Dharma calls for investing time and attention to work. The unspoken assurance of this is that results unmistakably follow work; one should therefore focus body, mind and soul on work and not worry needlessly about outcomes. Such a commitment towards work is enough to sustain one's Dharma towards self, family and society. We must do our work diligently with full ownership and commitment, so as to climb the ladders of corporate hierarchy faster and get more for our time invested in the form of better salary increments, bonus or promotions.

Dharma towards society

Most of us understand that giving back to the society can be in the form of charity, endowment to orphanages, old age homes, homes for children with special needs and NGOs working for the underprivileged, etc., once we have sufficiently done our duty towards self, family and work. While this is true, we can make a bigger change to our society by imparting the right financial

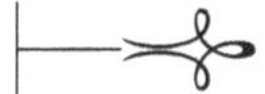

education to people around us so that the society as a whole progresses financially.

Today, in India, financial education is a big concern. A large majority of Indian households still park their money in fixed deposits, gold and real-estate. It is surprising that 2/3rd of our population invests in physical assets, like real estate or gold. Equity investments merely attract 16–17% of Indian savings. Gold is seen as a safe haven by Indians though in reality it performs well only in periods of uncertainty. Similarly, real estate has not given better returns than equity in the past. If one considers the quantum of interest paid on home loans, one will find that it actually offsets the appreciation in value of real estate, making it substantially less attractive than equity. An overwhelming proportion of financial savings and investments continue to flow into fixed income avenues. Bank deposits, government, and small savings schemes, like PPF, are the most popular fixed income destinations in the country. It is surprising that even money invested in mutual funds is largely (~60%) in fixed income funds. We Indians have always had a deep-rooted love for predictable returns. However, the good news is that this has somewhat changed in recent years. Decades ago, investing would mean the same as putting one's money in bank accounts and investing in equity was perceived to be only for the rich or for speculators. It must be noted that while equity can be volatile in the short term, in the long term, no other asset class can beat the real returns given by equity.

Conclusion

One's Dharma towards financial well-being is to discharge one's duty towards self, family, work and society in that order.

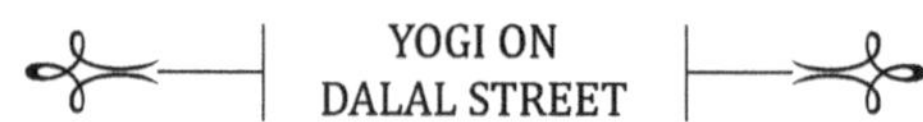

It is one's own Dharma, that one operates, from a standpoint of financial safety by ensuring a proper contingency plan, insurance cover and tax planning. After that, one must plan for financial goals for the family, be it a child's education, buying a home, retirement planning etc. One must discharge duties towards work with utmost sincerity so that one's time is well rewarded. And finally, one must engage in spreading the light of Vidya (knowledge). Teach people around the art of investing prudently with allocation to equity as an asset class, alleviate their fears about volatility involved and educate them about the risks and returns associated with investing in equities. This would help society to progress financially. If all of us are successful in discharging our four categories of Dharma mentioned above, then it would create a world where "Sarve Bhavantu Sukhinah" meaning "May all be happy and prosperous" is a reality.

Chapter 2

Gyana

GYANA

तत्रनिरतिशयंसर्वज्ञबीजम्

Tatra niratiśayaṁ sarvajña-bījam

In the Higher is the seed of all knowledge.

– 1.25 Patanjali Yoga Sutra

Gyana expresses itself in two ways in a Yoga investor. It is firstly a certainty of 'knowing', which comes from a careful study of the real world and not from hearsay or blind faith. The other quality of the Gyana Bhavna is that it expresses itself as an aggressive curiosity to know or understand more.

Gyana begins with awareness of one's physical, mental, emotional and spiritual selves. It embodies knowledge, mental alacrity, mindfulness, balance, coordination and concentration. Yoga Asanas involving concentration, balance, synchronization and coordination like Talasana are related to Gyana Bhava.

These Asanas help practise mindfulness at all levels - physical, mental, emotional and spiritual which then leads to the acquisition of wisdom, coordination and concentration.

It has been said that growth stops for an individual on the day one stops seeking knowledge. Dharma and Gyana go hand in hand. The defining feature of Dharma is Viveka or the process of differentiating right from wrong; it is not blind acceptance of a creed. One cannot differentiate between right and wrong if one has no Gyana. Dharma is, in fact, blind without Gyana, and Gyana without Dharma is directionless. Likewise, careful goal setting (Dharma) without meticulous knowledge backed execution (Gyana) of the action plan is meaningless.

Knowledge rooted in painstaking research is the most powerful pillar of success for an investment. The chances of success for any

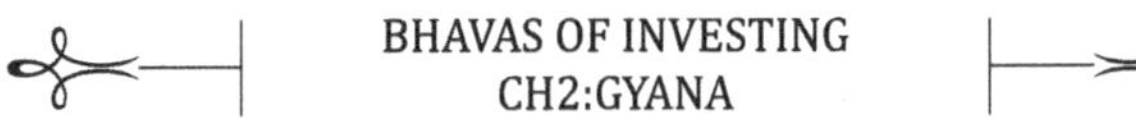

investment made after thorough background checks and knowledge of the market is far higher than one made without any research or knowledge. Investing without knowledge deteriorates into mere speculation.

Gyana starts with knowing oneself well first and then identifying which asset classes suits one's financial goals the most.

Know thyself and know the companies one is investing in

An old financial thumb rule says the percentage of investments in risky assets should be '100 minus your Age'. However, this rule may not be applicable to all individual investors. For instance, a retired individual who is well settled in life and has limited liability can have a high exposure to equities because they can take more risks. In contrast, a young investor who has many responsibilities like honouring one's EMIs for an education loan or a home loan may not have the leeway to sustain high exposure to a risky asset class. This example would substantiate the fact that age is no longer a basis for defining one's exposure to equities. It is risk profiling that must be considered instead.

I. Know thyself

स्वाध्यायादिष्टदेवतासंप्रयोगः ॥ ४४ ॥

svadhyayat ishta devata sampraYogah

By the study of scriptures, and of oneself, the consciousness is united with the desired

-2.44 Patanjali Yoga Sutra

Svadhyaya literally means self-study. Similarly, before investing investors should know about their goals and their risk-taking

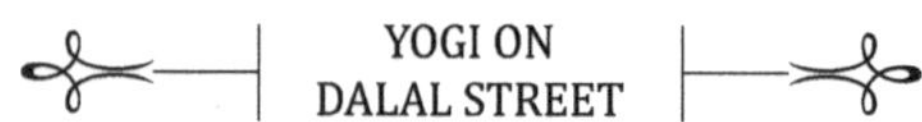

capacity. An archer has tremendous concentration and balance when they are aiming for the bull's eye. They have the right knowledge, skill and will power to target the centre of the board. Moreover, they are aware of their body and their hand-eye coordination is in sync.

So as to know about oneself, one needs to ask themselves the following questions:

- How well do I know myself as an investor?
- What are my financial goals and what is the time-frame within which these goals have to be met?
- How stable is my income, and my spouse's? Do I have any older dependents?
- How much of my savings are in traditional fixed-income earning instruments and how much of my money am I willing to invest (periodically or in one go)?
- How much risk am I willing to take with my financial decisions? What is the average rate of returns I expect from my portfolio over the next 10 years?
- How much is my exposure to equities? Should I raise my equity allocation?

The answer to all the above questions will give one a clear picture about their financial goals, their investments and risk-taking ability. Risk profiling is very important as the more risk one is willing to take, the more returns they stand to earn. One's risk profile captures the real them, their anxieties, expectations and aspirations.

For an investor to correctly analyse their risk profile, there are 2 things they must be well aware of internally:

1. The amount of risk they are at ease with i.e. *risk tolerance*
2. The amount of risk they are capable of taking i.e. *risk capacity*

One needs to attain a proper balance between personal comfort and personal competence in matters of risk-taking. The above two parameters vary from individual to individual and are subjective in nature.

These two things need to be matched with the 3rd parameter i.e. the *actual risk* that the investment calls for, towards achievement of one's goals.

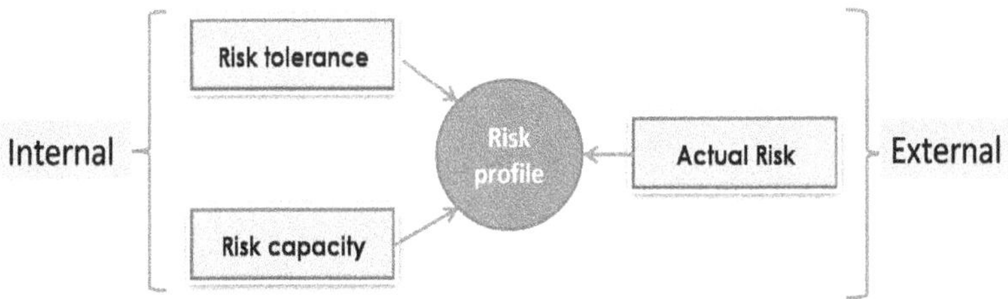

Once a match is achieved between all three parameters mentioned, an investor's risk profile is fully defined. The two internal parameters act like constraints to define the returns which an investor achieves. If one aspires for a higher return, the internal parameters would need to be altered.

The basic expectation of an investor is to maximize one's returns keeping one's risk as low as possible. From the bouquet of investment avenues available at the behest of the investor, they have to form a portfolio keeping an eye on their risk tolerance and risk taking capacity. Debt instruments, bank fixed deposits or savings accounts offer a low real return along with a low risk as the cash flows are predictable and unlikely to change unless a major disruption happens to the economy. Similarly, gold and real estate, with all the hassles of being physical assets, are likely to offer slightly higher real return over fixed income instruments. Equity returns, on other hand, have historically beaten other asset classes by wide margins and have the potential to repeat the same in a growing economy. The risks associated with Equities can very well be minimised if the investment horizon is long, say 10–15 years. Thus even if an investor has low risk tolerance and risk handling capacity, their overall risk can be minimised by extending the investment horizon. All these three parameters when coupled with equities would offer superior real returns for an investor.

II. Know the sectors and companies one invests in

After assessing one's own risk profile, it is important to understand one's target investment. While buying a TV or refrigerator, a conscious consumer will compare various features of different brands before arriving at a buying decision. However, the same person would behave differently while investing, and will take impulsive decisions without confirming the credentials of the source of the information about the investment. One must make a conscious effort to research an investment. If they do not have the resources to research, approach a financial advisor or invest in mutual funds or subscribe using the SIP route.

The risk involved with investing in direct equity differs based on the market capitalisation of the companies. Market capitalisation (cap) can be defined as the current market price multiplied by outstanding number of shares. The higher the market cap, the lower the risk. The market cap can be categorised into large cap, mid cap or small cap. The top 100 companies in terms of market capitalisation will come under the large cap segment, while the 101st-250th firms will be mid-cap. From the 251st company onwards, in terms of market capitalisation, will be small-cap.

The stocks of large cap companies are considered safe as they are mature companies and have a large market share in their respective sectors. Midcaps are relatively smaller companies and may or may not be market leaders in their sectors, whereas small caps are still smaller ones, in terms of market size and market share. Given the size of the company and economic growth opportunities, mid and small cap companies are likely to have better prospects for growth.

Having understood the risks associated, based on market cap, now the job at hand is to identify fundamentally sound stocks with great future potential. It is important that one learns about the company, its product or service, and studies its management and financial reports to get first hand information about the investment one is intending to make. In other words, one must carry out an analysis of a company before investing in it for the long term.

In-depth analysis of companies involves a close look at the qualitative and quantitative parameters. Once an investor understands the dynamics of a particular industry, it becomes fairly easy to track the companies in that industry.

Analysis involves taking a top-down or bottom-up approach. In a top-down approach, an investor looks at the 'big picture' first. Starting from the improving economic conditions, say reducing interest rates, one moves down to the sectors that are going to benefit due to a specific economic variable, like automobile industry or the housing sector. Subsequently, within these sectors the investor identifies companies that are strongly positioned against their peers and poised to grow in the future.

In the bottom-up approach, the investor directly zeros in on the target companies and subsequently, takes note of the broad economic conditions. Here, the investor identifies the company first and then takes into account certain company specific developments, say management change or relative undervaluation of the company compared to its peer set, or the launch of a new product which is expected to give the company an advantage.

Conclusion

Life is fraught with dangers for the one blinded by Avidya (ignorance). What eyes are to the human body, Gyana is to investment. Gyana is the light that illuminates all roads one walks on in one's life. In this light, one can decide from a safe distance whether to proceed or retreat or to undertake a course correction on one's investment journey. To make sound investment decisions one has to understand products, markets, business cycles, and policy frameworks thoroughly. Without Gyana, even operating in the market becomes a herculean task. With Gyana, the chances of success improve manifold. The key to situating oneself in Gyana Bhavna is to stoke one's natural curiosity so one develops an insatiable appetite for knowledge.

Knowledge in, knowledge out.

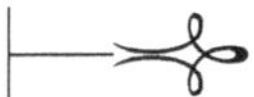

Chapter 3

Vairagya

VAIRAGYA

अभ्यासवैराग्याअभ्यांतन्निरोधः ॥ १२ ॥

abhyāsa-Vairagya-ābhyāṁ tan-nirodhaḥ

All dancing and miming of the mind can be stopped with correct practice and detachment.

– 1.12 Patanjali Yoga Sutra

Abhyasa and Vairagya are companion practices. Abhyasa is cultivating the truth. Vairagya is the letting go of attachments and aversions that lead away from the truth. Vairagya is the state of dispassion. It is an ability to objectively visualize everything, including one's body and mind. The practitioner is in a completely relaxed mode, watching everything as a third party or from a bird's eye view. One adopts an attitude of humility, detachment and objectivity, depicting a surrender to some higher force. All the forward bends, relaxation postures in Asanas like Yoga Mudra are covered under Vairagya Bhava.

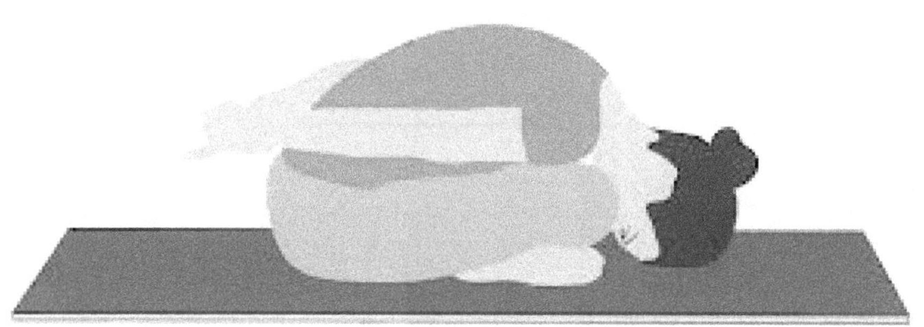

One who exudes Vairagya Bhavna steps back and surrenders to the market forces once they are done with due diligence on an investment opportunity. This is a Bhavna that all great masters of investing display in varying degrees. Having identified an opportunity and investing in it, the investor ignores short-term price fluctuations, enters a state of self-imposed inactivity and detachment, and refrains from checking the portfolio daily. Such dispassion is a lesson to all who wish to invest in stocks for profit. This is especially true for any equity-linked investments either made directly in stocks or in mutual funds. The returns could be slow initially, however dividends along with capital appreciation snowball into higher returns as fruits of compounding accrue.

An investor who wants to deepen the state of Vairagya within, in letter and spirit, can do so only after one is convinced about the business potential of the intended investment, its growth prospects and longevity along with management integrity. One then tries to purchase the business at attractive valuations, irrespective of market conditions. The companies in focus need to have strong entry barriers, may be, in terms of brand value or positioning and a competitive advantage over peers. The business model and the organisational structure should be so robust that the company should be able to tide over competitive forces and other hurdles. In essence, for the long term, buy stocks of companies that have great processes, culture, products etc., which give a sustainable business advantage. Having bought the intended business with a sufficient margin of safety, the investor is well-positioned to get into the state of Vairagya and enjoy the power of compounding.

What is compounding?

Investments under compounding offer far higher returns compared to normal interest rates because the baseline from which the interest is calculated rises every year in a 'compounding situation'. Ideally, on investing in year one, one should receive returns at the end of the year, which should then be added up in the principal for the next year. Thus the base increases for the second year. At the end of the second year, the return would be on a larger amount than in the first year. This is because the balance at the end of year one would be the principal plus the interest earned in year one. Thus, compounding offers a multiplier effect. As the interest earned by the initial investment also earns an interest in subsequent years, the value of the investment grows at a faster rate (along an exponential curve) vis-à-vis an arithmetic rate (along a straight line). It must be remembered that compounding is a long-term strategy. When invested over the long term, the real fruits of compounding can be realised. Even modest returns can generate real wealth, if given enough time.

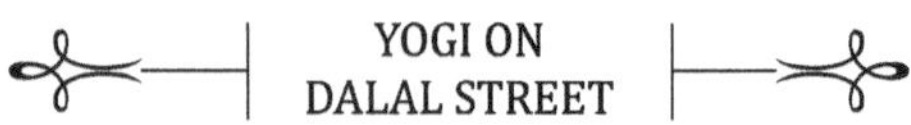

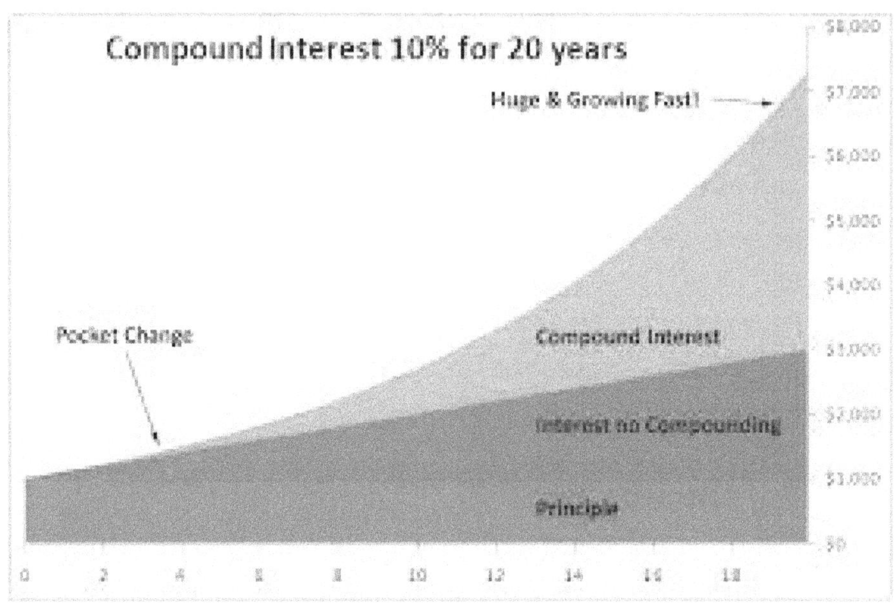

The power of compounding

Having selected a bunch of stocks for investment, one should buy and hold them, to give the investments an adequate amount of time to appreciate northwards from the level of purchase. Stocks are ruled by the power of compounding. It is due to this phenomenon that one sees an investment appreciate in multiples over a period of time.

Compounding is akin to the snowball effect. Albert Einstein made an apt statement on compound interest when he called it 'the eighth wonder of the world' and remarked, "He, who understands it, earns it and he who doesn't, pays it'. The sooner one identifies a stock and holds it for long, the higher is the return.

Basic rules to get rich by using the power of compounding:

a. Start early: The earlier one starts, the longer the corpus gets to multiply.

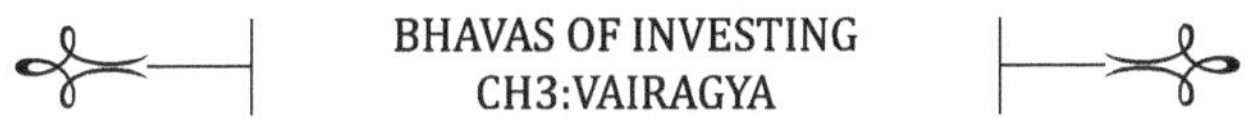

b. Inculcate the regular investment habit: Disciplined and regular investments in the form of SIP should be done even if the amounts are small.

c. Patiently watch the investments grow: Do not disturb the investment; compounding works if it is allowed to grow. The longer the money is left to compound, the bigger the fortune one accumulates.

The following are the key factors that affect the returns from compounding:

1. The annual rate of interest: The higher the annual interest, the faster the investment grows. For example if an investor invests Rs 1,000 in an investment vehicle that guarantees a return of 8% per annum, the investment by the end of 20 years would be Rs. 4,927. However, if one invests the same amount at 12% for 20 years, the investment would balloon into Rs. 10,893. Just by increasing the rate by 4%, the corpus more than doubles in the same period.

2. Period of Investment: The longer one remains invested without making withdrawals, the more effective is the compounding. If one's rate of return is 12%, one would double their investment amount in 6 years, triple it within 9 ½ years and quadruple it in 12 years. The 1st multiplier happens in 6 years, then in 3 ½ years, then in 2 ½ years and the time to multiply one's wealth keeps decreasing over a period of time. So, the longer the better!

3. Initial amount invested: In the previous example, if one were to place Rs. 10,000 instead of Rs. 1,000, the amount one would have earned via compounding interest would have also been 10 times as much.

Despite the simplicity of compounding interest, it is through sheer patience and discipline that one is able to fully maximise the power of compounding. An investor should possess Vairagya or dispassion, and have the fortitude to hold on to the stocks in one's portfolio and ride the cycles of earnings and hence, price fluctuations, and give the stock sufficient time to reach its highs in terms of business and price/valuations.

One must learn to accept changes that impact their investment negatively in the short run and acknowledge them as a part of the journey. In investing, small losses and downfalls should not shake one up. Even though short-term losses are inevitable, they are more than compensated for in the long term, provided one has done their due diligence before entering the stock. Despite the various ups and downs in the short run, the Sensex has grown from 100 in 1979 to 58991 in March 2023, giving a CAGR of ~13.6% despite short term ups and downs. Following is the growth in the index since inception.

As we discussed in Abhinivesha, nothing is permanent and everything is up for change. One should adopt Anitya Bhavna to

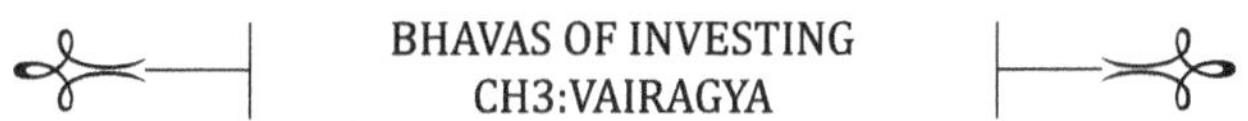

get used to change, instead of getting distracted, and concentrate on the BIG picture. One must be mindful of these few golden rules to deepen the Vairagya Bhavna in one's financial planning journey -

Equity markets will never give one linear returns and in the short-term, there may be various market events that can 'correct' equity prices.

Most people tend to overreact to news in equity markets that are only temporary in nature. It is important to detach oneself from noise.

Volatility is the nature of the market. One cannot avoid it.

If the investment is meaningful from a long-term perspective, the opportunity will continue to remain a good one, even in future.

One should not focus on instant returns, and should not change one's investment decisions based on short-term returns.

Vairagya is detachment not renunciation:

Remember, Vairagya Bhavna is not the same as renunciation. Vairagya does not involve the giving up of the world but of being in it yet not being affected by it. The classical symbol of Vairagya is the lotus flower that grows in water but remains dry. Investors steeped in Vairagya look carefully at all the reports they can lay their hands on and decide on the basis of cold facts. They do not allow the noise in the market to lead them astray.

It is imperative for an investor to periodically watch and critically analyse the performance of the company or portfolio in order to check if the investment is moving in the right direction by comparing it to benchmarks laid down at the time of investment.

Conclusion

Cultivating detachment in our lives usually means cultivating an attitude of humility and surrender. Yoga Asanas which impart Vairagya Bhavna include forward bends and twists. These postures encourage us to surrender and relax into the pose: if one is tensing their muscles and pushing hard, it's more difficult to succeed with forward bends and twists, but if one lets go and surrenders to the pose without trying to push, one will often find that one can bend just a little bit farther, twist just a little bit deeper. Similarly, in the equity markets, once one has selected the stocks to invest in, after proper analysis, one should surrender oneself to the volatilities in the market, develop objectivity and observe the power of compounding. Unless there is a fundamental change in the core values of the companies one has invested in, one should be able to hold them for years. One should ignore the fluctuations in the paper value of their holdings. If one has bought companies with strong foundations, one can relax and watch compounding do its work.

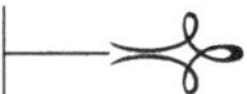

Chapter 4

Aishwarya

Aishwarya

Aishwarya is the expression of abundance and wellbeing; a culmination or flowering of the three preceding Bhavas of Dharma, Gyana and Vairagya. The Bhavna of Aishwarya is not invoked in a person on gaining wealth or prosperity, it is the necessary condition for attracting wealth in one's life. From the perspective of Yoga investing, the outcomes we experience outside are but the consequence of the shifts that we experience within. Aishwarya is experienced as a feeling of achievement and satisfaction along with humility. All this adds great confidence to one's personality. The components of Aishwarya are confidence, self-reliance, sense of achievement, effort, will-power, fortitude, freedom, strength and forbearance. These qualities allow one to experience a beautiful flow of life.

All backbends or movements in Yoga like Bhujangasana evoke a sense of uplifting or achievement in an individual.

When one performs one's Dharma or duty to practice financial planning and selects the right financial advisor, investing using the power of Gyana or knowledge and detaching oneself from the noise of the market with Vairagya, can enable one to experience Aishwarya Bhava, which is a necessary condition for achieving great wealth and happiness. Thus, one can only attain Aishwarya in the equity markets if one has experienced the first three Bhavas. We must realise that it is a long, continuous and joyous process.

Life without money is a difficult one. The lack of money affects a person in a hundred ways. It narrows down one's choices and impacts the standard of living for one's family. Having adequate money is a necessity. Once one's needs are taken care of, they can focus on things that are important in life that bring one happiness. It is, therefore, not about being money-minded but being mindful of one's money. What Yoga taught us thousands of years ago has been stated afresh by the psychologist Abraham Maslow. His 'hierarchy of needs' describes the stages of psychological growth in humans that conclude in the stage of self-actualisation. To reach that ultimate state, one has to transcend a hierarchy of physiological needs like

1. safety, 2. love and belonging and 3. self-esteem. Maslow's theory suggests that the most basic level of needs must be met before the individual feels the urge (or focuses one's motivation upon) secondary or higher level needs.

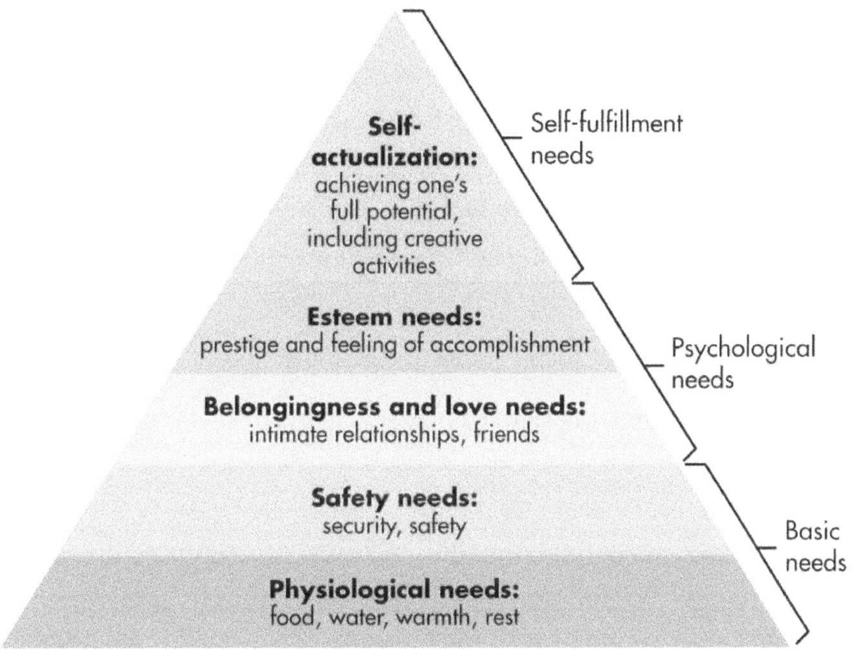

Golden rules to achieve Aishwarya in equity markets

The following steps must be taken to ensure investment discipline:

One should perform Dharma of goal-based financial planning after considering all short, medium and long-term goals.

One should do due diligence before investing. One must also keep a margin of safety while investing and never invest based on hearsay. Proper research should be done well before investing and the investor should invest on the basis of one's goals, investment horizon and risk profile.

Investors should adopt a 'buy and hold' strategy with periodic reviews. The less frequently one tracks the market and checks one's portfolio, the less likely one is to react emotionally to the natural ups and downs of the equity market. For most investors, checking the portfolio in a structured manner (during quarterly results of a company or some important event) is sufficient.

One must think deeply before taking long-term investment decisions. Losing one day's return will not matter if one wants to hold the equity for 10 years. When one sees signs of panic or euphoria, the best advice would be to wait for another day. If the investment is meaningful from a long-term perspective, the opportunity will continue to remain a good one, even in future.

One should have appropriate asset allocation, and rebalance their portfolio periodically.

Invest at regular intervals.

When one succeeds, one should evaluate which of the actions contributed to the success, and which ones did not. Investors claim the credit for successes that have occurred by chance. They should avoid rationalizations when they fail. They shouldn't exaggerate the role of bad luck in their failures.

Bliss of being in Aishwarya state

Aishwarya state in investing helps one to live a financially secure and fruitful life due to the following reasons:

Managing Income: With financial planning, managing income becomes a matter of habit. It helps one understand how much money one will need for savings, tax payments and other monthly expenditures.

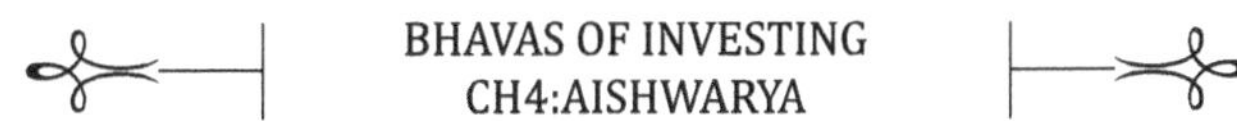

Better Cash Flows: It increases one's cash flows as one meticulously tracks their spending patterns and expenses. Tax planning, prudent spending and careful budgeting will help one to keep more of one's hard earned cash.

Increased Capital: An increase in cash flow, automatically leads to higher allocation of money towards investments, which in turn assures higher capital that improves one's overall financial well-being.

Family Security: Providing for one's family's financial security is an important aspect of the financial planning process. Having the proper insurance coverage and estate planning in place can provide peace of mind for investors and their loved ones.

Right Investments: A proper financial plan considers one's personal circumstances, objectives and risk tolerance. It guides one to choose the right types of investments to fit their needs, personality and goals. It helps them harness the power of equity in the long-term to beat inflation and tax.

Ensures standard of living: The savings created through good planning can prove a safety cushion in difficult times. For example, a family breadwinner can make sure there is enough insurance coverage to replace any lost income, if they find themself unable to work.

Cushion for emergency: It helps one to be prepared for a rainy day. Sudden financial changes can throw one off track and it is advisable to stay prepared for such eventualities by having some investments with high liquidity.

Financial understanding: Better financial understanding can be achieved when measurable financial goals are set, the effects of decisions understood, and results reviewed. This gives one a whole new approach to one's budget and improves their control over their financial life.

Balances assets and liabilities: A nice 'cushion' in the form of assets is desirable. But many assets come with liabilities attached. So, it becomes important to determine the real value of an asset. The knowledge of settling or cancelling liabilities comes with the understanding of one's finances. The overall process helps build assets that don't become a burden in the future.

Conclusion

Aishwarya Bhavna places the state of one's finances at a level that helps them not only practice the Dharma towards oneself and one's family but elevates them to a plane where they are able to contribute to society and humanity in general. With effort, all these Bhavas can be awakened till we experience Aishwarya in all its glory.

Module 3

Gunas of Investing

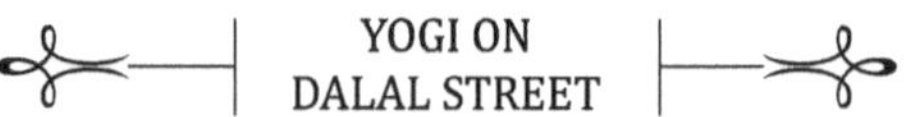

Preface

तततःकृताथनिंपरिणामक्रमसमाप्तिर्गुणानाम्

When knowledge dawns, the dance of the Gunas comes to a standstill.

Tataḥ kṛtārthānaṁ pariṇāma-krama-samāptir-Gunanām

– 4.32 Patanjali Yoga Sutra

The Sanskrit word 'Guna' is an approximation of the expression 'defining quality'. Yoga considers Prakriti or nature to be composed of the three Gunas:

1. Tamas
2. Rajas and
3. Sattva

Every material (made of matter) that exists in the phenomenal world is composed of these three Gunas, including our body. These three Gunas create the world of multiplicity. As the Gunas are engaged in a perpetual activity, one of three Gunas dominates our being at any particular time while the other two Gunas await their roles. An investor is no exception to the interplay of Gunas; depending on the Guna dominating the body, mind and intellect, they think, analyse and arrive at decisions. In the pages that follow we explore the role of Gunas in investment behaviour, and attempt to utilise this ancient Yoga knowledge for wealth creation.

So, how does one understand how the Gunas are working in their body? The days when one just can't get themselves up or awaken from sleep, and feel unmotivated and bereft of energy, one is in a state of inertia dominated by Tamas. Similarly, an investor in the state of Tamas or Tamasic investor typically refuses to walk the

extra mile in efforts to grow one's wealth as they do not have the energy to think or act vigorously.

When one feels energetic or hyperactive all day, and finds it hard to stop, one is in a state of energetic restlessness where the Rajas Guna reigns. An investor in whom Rajas dominate has more energy than one needs and this makes them restless. A Rajasic investor will rarely invest in instruments that lock the money for long periods as they do not have the patience to wait.

When tranquility prevails, and one feels calm and clear and appears to do much with an economical spend of effort, one is in a state of harmony between inertia and energy called Sattva.

When Sattva overrides Rajas and Tamas, concentration and meditation are easy. When Rajas rule, one can sit in a meditative posture but the mind is busy. When there is preponderance of Tamas, the desire for action disappears. For such a person, even the thought of meditation may not arise in the mind.

Let us understand these Gunas with greater clarity.

Tamas

Tamas is a state of darkness, inertia, inactivity and materiality. It is rooted in ignorance or Avidya. A state of mind ruled by Tamas is considered to be the lowest among the three Gunas as it represents lethargy. A Tamasic state is a state of lazy inaction. A Tamasic person tends to have low involvement with what is happening around them.

Despite it being 'an inactive state', Tamas is essential for the well being of an individual. You must be wondering how. The reason is 'rest'. Rest or sleep is necessary for a living creature to recuperate its energies, hence periodic dominance of Tamas is essentially called for. Thus, being essential, Tamas cannot be done away with but should be actively regulated. Also, its influence should be allowed within a prescribed limit, not more nor less.

Rajas

Rajas is a state of action and movement. It is the energy of change, distinguished by passion, desire, effort and pain. A Rajasic person has an active mind, full of vigour. They are all observant; their mind perceives minute details, analyses them and uses the knowledge to their benefit. A Rajasic personality has a hyperactive mind that craves high levels of activity. If this energy is channelised properly, it can earn laurels, if not, it leads to destruction. It is the channelised Rajasic trait/ Guna that leads a person to prosperity.

Sattva

Sattva is a state of harmony, balance, joy and stable intellect. Sattva as a Guna exists at the point of balance between Rajas and Tamas, combining the energy of Rajas with the stability of Tamas. Sattva Guna is therefore the most desired of the Gunas. Since it is the mode of goodness, being purer than the others, it is illuminating and full of wellbeing.

Sattvic investors are free from lethargy induced by Tamas or excessive energy brought about by Rajas. They are calm, collected and clear-headed. They think clearly and their actions are also guided by this clarity.

If one thinks that one is not Sattvic enough as an investor, there is good news. Everybody possesses all the 3 Gunas including Sattva and one can consciously steer one's body/mind/intellect towards a specific Guna through the discipline of Yoga.

Page is for illustration of Gunas through Venn Diagram

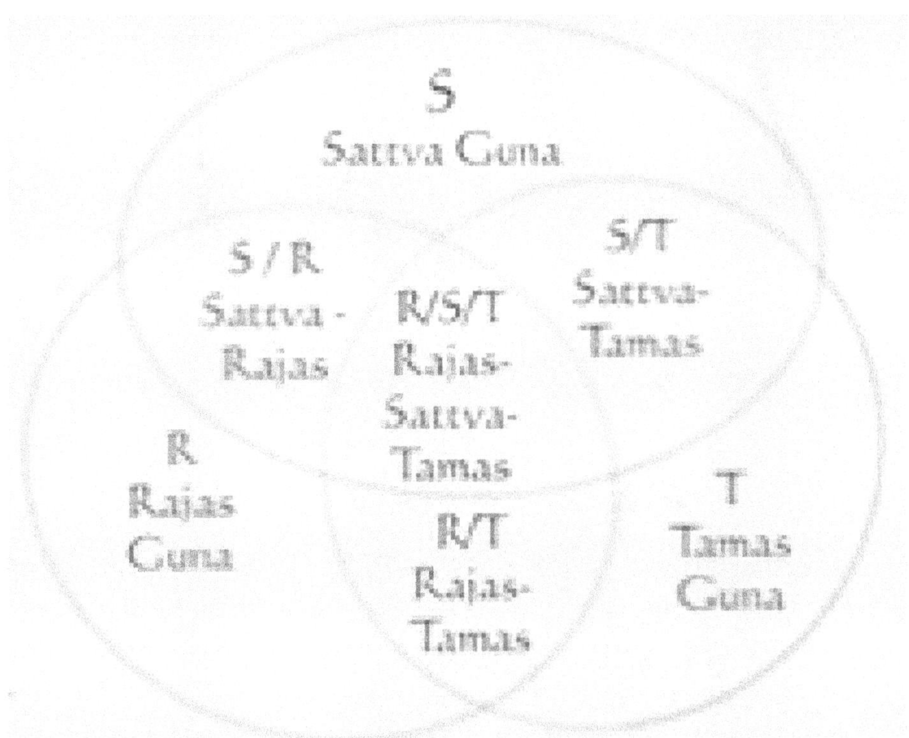

According to the Yoga Sutra, human beings, due to their higher level of consciousness, possess the unique ability to consciously work upon these Gunas to increase or decrease their effect in the mind, thereby creating a Sattvic mind. The same Sattvic mind beholds the world outside with great clarity. When utilised for wealth creation, it is moved neither by the vagaries of the market nor by hearsay. A Sattvic mind operates from a space of poise and judges on the basis of facts presented before it. Sattva is therefore the most desirable Guna for all aspiring investors.

Let us now see how the dance of the three Gunas impacts the art and skill of investing.

Chapter 1

Tamas

TAMAS

तमस्त्वज्ञानजंविद्धिमोहनंसर्वदेहिनाम् |

प्रमादालस्यनिद्राभिस्तन्निबध्नातिभारत || 8 ||

Tamas tv ajñāna-jaṁ viddhi, mohanaṁ sarva-dehinām,

pramādālasya-Nidrabhis, tan nibadhnāti bhārata

O son of Bharata, the mode of darkness, born of ignorance, is the delusion of all embodied living entities. The results of this mode are madness, indolence and sleep, which bind the conditioned soul.

– 14.8 Bhagavad Gita

Tamas is the least desirable of the three Gunas. It dominates the body, mind and intellect of individuals under the spell of Avidya or ignorance. A Tamasic psyche refuses to budge from its comfort zone. It is satisfied with what comes its way in the form of rewards and generally keeps its money idle in savings accounts.

Save for a rainy day, goes an old adage. While saving may have worked in the past, today, one needs to invest. If one believes that saving and investing imply the same thing, think again.

Saving doesn't necessarily provide returns, and whatever one saves can only meet one's short-term needs. On the other hand, investing provides real returns. It also helps one grow their money and provides them with financial security and means for goal fulfillment.

In Yoga parlance, Tamas means inactivity or inertia, which is also reflected in the term savings. Merely saving something does not grow one's investment. It lets the money stay where it is without any growth. In the context of investing, Tamas is most undesirable as a preponderance of Tamas in investment behaviour expresses itself as a reluctance to go beyond mere savings.

As a Tamas Pradhan person, one has a limited understanding about investments and is happy letting money stay in a Bank Savings account itself or continues to park it in traditional asset classes like bank FDs and gold. Such people are oblivious of different avenues for investment and do not take the initiative to manage their finances. They seldom look beyond the day to day needs; have no plans for the future, neither for themself nor for their family. Thus, they end up making a minimum return on their money, which could also turn out to be negative in real terms, after accounting for inflation. They are bound by inertia and do not like moving out of their comfort zone to gain Vidya about investing. They harbour Dvesha (aversion) and Abhinivesha (fear of losing all), which keeps them away from the ever volatile equity market.

Is Tamas always bad?

Despite the poor rate of returns on FDs and gold, they should still form an essential part of one's overall investment portfolio. However, one must be mindful of the allocation. A disproportionately higher skew would mean underperformance of the portfolio and the converse may mean an overly aggressive or risky portfolio.

Being in a state of Tamas may not be beneficial to anyone in the long run. One must, however, understand that it is necessary to take advantage of this state to some extent. Again taking the example of sleep- it is a state of pure inactivity that is essential for the periodic rejuvenation of the body. However, too much or too little sleep can potentially disturb one's productive working hours. So, Tamas is not to be eliminated from one's portfolio but harnessed for one's profit.

So, how much is too much when it comes to Tamas in investment?

Well, that would depend on one's current risk profile. Let us consider someone both young and unmarried with no familial responsibilities and with a decent salary, or an old retired person earning a pension with close to no responsibilities and sufficient disposable surpluses. The portfolios of such persons would call for minimal allocation of funds to FDs or gold and maximum allocation to equity. On the other hand, if someone is nearing retirement or is the single earning member of a family with too many dependents and/or with clears short-term goals that call for fixed sums of money, they should allocate a higher amount to FD investments.

Breaking the hold of Tamas

The problem with Tamasic people is that they stay in the comfort zone of simply parking their money in fixed deposits, gold and real-estate, as their parents did. The predominant Tamas Guna can be regressive in the long run. Therefore, one has to break free of one's comfort zone and look at contemporary investment options even within fixed income products.

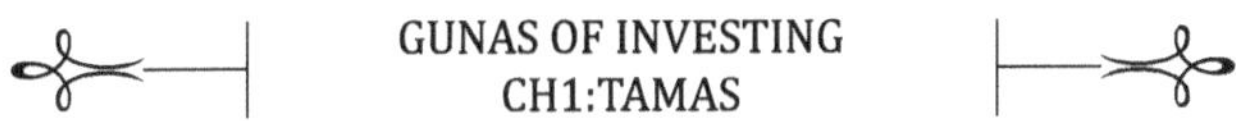

To start with, the Tamasic investor has to shake themself off their lethargy, gain some Gyana (knowledge) and learn more about better investment products, which offer higher returns over traditional investment avenues. Instead of savings accounts or FDs, one can have a look at Debt Mutual funds which include liquid funds, short term funds and ultra short term funds. These types of funds offer fairly predictable and stable returns and have negligible volatility; the returns are substantially higher than the traditional counterparts. Similarly, instead of investing in physical gold one can look at options like Gold Exchange Traded Funds (ETFs) or Sovereign Gold bonds. Gold ETFs can be easily bought and sold on the exchange just like stocks and they mirror the price of gold. As opposed to physical gold in the form of jewellery, Gold ETFs relieve one from concerns about safety and maintenance or loss due to impurity. In the case of real-estate, similarly, investing in REITs can help the Tamasic investor reap the benefits of real estate investments along with the ease and advantages of investing in stocks. REITs have historically provided investors dividend-based income, competitive market performance, transparency, liquidity, inflation protection and portfolio diversification. Moreover, the performance of REITs is not correlated to real estate prices.

All these contemporary forms of traditional asset classes have taken away a lot of disadvantages associated with them. If Tamasic investors want to elevate themselves towards Sattva, they must realise that the road from Tamas to Sattva passes through Rajas. Deep seated patterns of attachment to a particular asset class, stagnation of confining one's surplus to savings and not investing in the equity market must be broken. It is important to grasp that equity is finally a superior asset class when it comes to long-term investing. We must, therefore, make an attempt to move towards it. Even if one cannot actively invest in equity markets, there are other

avenues that allow us to participate in equity with relatively low risk and effort. Firstly, one can start by investing in Gold ETFs, Debt mutual funds or REITS. Slowly, one can then progress to passive forms of equity like Exchange Traded Funds (ETFs) that mirror the performance of indices like Nifty or Bank Nifty and provide the same returns as the index. ETFs allow individuals who wish to invest small amounts of money and reap the benefits of diversification to participate in the equity market. Also, one can choose to invest through **mutual fund schemes.** Mutual Fund houses deploy the investor's money in various stocks or debt instruments depending on the objective of the fund. The deployment of money is based on professional expertise of a fund manager. This option also allows investors the twin advantages of an actively managed portfolio (unlike ETFs) by experts and that too with small amounts of money.

Newton's first law of motion states, 'An object at rest tends to stay at rest until and unless it is acted upon by an unbalanced external force'. While this law of Physics applies to physical objects, Yoga philosophy states that the human mind is malleable (clay-like), and it possesses the potential to reach higher states. The heightened activity that the rise of Rajas Guna brings in a person enables one to let go of inertia. However, the force required for this 'rising' or change has to come from within. Therefore, to get out of the Tamasic state, some inner fire of Rajas is necessary. Once a person is able to maintain a balance between Tamas and Rajas, one can make Sattva predominant.

Conclusion

Excess Tamas is undesirable as it leads one to ignorance, delusion and sufferings. Therefore, it is one's Dharma towards oneself to remove oneself from the state of Tamas and take calibrated

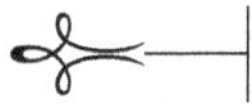 

steps to reach Sattva. One needs to evoke Gyana Bhavna and consciously take steps to shed Tamas progressively. If equity is too overpowering to begin with, one may take baby steps by looking at more contemporary options of investing in traditional asset classes using Gold ETFs, Debt mutual funds or REITS. In equity, one may participate passively through the ETFs or equity mutual funds route that requires minimum intervention once invested.

Tamas are necessary but one must modulate it to strike the right balance. Very much like our sleep schedule i.e. sleep corners $1/4^{th}$ to $1/3^{rd}$ of the 24 hours of the day, the low return assets like FDs and gold should ideally be not more than 25–30% of one's portfolio. It is very useful to arrive at what works for oneself to get out of the Tamasic state.

Life begins at the end of one's comfort zone. So, one must step out of one's comfort zone and stay awake to one's finances. One should not neglect them.

Chapter 2

Rajas

RAJAS

रजोरागात्मकंविद्धितृष्णासङ्गसमुद्भवम् ।

तन्निबध्नातिकौन्तेयकर्मसङ्गेनदेहिनम् ॥ 7 ॥

Rajo Ragatmakaṁ viddhi tṛṣhṇā-saṅga-samudbhavam, tan nibadhnāti kaunteya karma-saṅgena dehinam

O Arjun, Rajas Guna is of the nature of passion. It arises from worldly desires and affections, and binds the soul through attachment to fruitive actions.

– 14.7 Bhagavad Gita

Rajas is the Guna of excitability that gives the impetus to achieve worldly aims. It is necessary to inject energy in those weighed down by the heaviness of Tamas Guna. Yogis use Rajas to pull themselves out of a state of sloth brought about by Tamas. Rajas is an aggressive Guna found widely among active equity traders who want their money to be in constant movement. They do not like passive forms of investing like fixed deposits, gold or real estate and they trade actively in equity markets. They get a thrill from trading in equity markets in the short term. The word trading is consciously being used here and not investing as the intent behind trading is to generate quick returns in the short term, irrespective

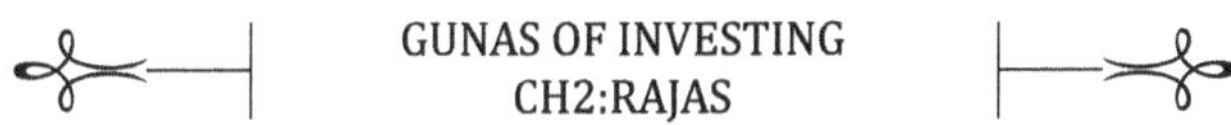

of the direction taken by the market, as opposed to investing that aims to grow wealth over the long term. Traders' mindsets revolve around getting maximum returns in minimum time by continuously monitoring price movements and participating in the flow. They seek arbitrage across markets, while taking minimal risk.

A trader doesn't go through the fundamentals of a company in detail as an investor does. A trader doesn't have the virtue of patience. Traders are only focused on 'what's happening now, and how can I profit from it'. They are constantly on the lookout for short term opportunities for quick money-making. A trader typically trades in leveraged products like intraday, futures and options.

Let us explain these concepts in brief. Intraday means buying and selling of stocks the same day. Derivative trading includes instruments like futures and options. These instruments derive their value from an underlying asset which can be stocks, indices, commodities, currencies, etc. They are simply contracts between two or more parties. The value of such a contract is determined by changes or fluctuations in the asset from which it derives its value. One may refer to a finance book or read online to get details of the same.

The question arises whether trading in equity markets is a good idea or not. The answer is not a straightforward yes or no. It actually depends on 'who you are', as a person. If one is high on Rajas or energy and is a risk taker, if numbers and chart patterns engage one's interest, then one should probably explore trading in equity markets.

Take the example of cricket. Both test matches and T-20 tournaments are two very different variants of the same game. Some players are a better fit for T-20 but not so much for test matches and vice versa. A test match requires technique and patience, where more than a run-rate, staying power on the crease and not losing wickets early matters. However, T-20 requires aggression, right from the first ball. The scoreboard must keep moving, no matter what.

Similarly, trading and investing are two very different variants of participating in equity markets. One must know who one is before one chooses their path.

The energy that a Rajasic person possesses has to be properly channelised, in a disciplined manner, to get the desired results. Thus a successful Rajasic person should have a backing of Vidya (knowledge) with least possible Asmita/ ego. Rajasic traders should acknowledge that the markets are above the individual and hence, befriend ego to make the most of it. They should not have Raga (attachments) to any specific asset class or equity and trade based on their defined chart-patterns and rule engine. Disciplined traders do not think twice before cutting short their positions, if the outcome is not in their favour, or they try to make the best of an opportunity that turns out to be favourable. Rajasic people live by the day; they are seldom influenced by the past and rarely care about what the future holds for them.

Novice traders typically end up trading in something based on hearsay as they have limited knowledge on the strategies of trading and they lack planning. Typically, novice traders buy a stock at the fag-end of its run up and when the stock reverses, fear creeps in when the stock goes lower and lower. Finally the pain becomes too much to bear so they sell taking a huge loss. This can be attributed largely to the failure to incorporate stop losses in their trades. A stop loss is basically the predetermined price at which one decides to cut one's loss. The idea is to have a

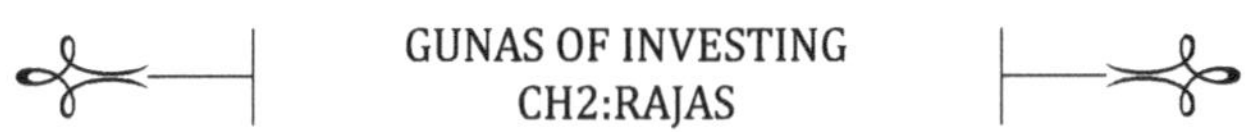

decent trading strategy and the mental discipline to stick with it. Traders should decide on the time horizon, stop loss and target price to book profits before entering into a trade. Then they must trade it according to the plan that they have decided. Remember that they have devised a plan before they got into the trade when their emotions were stable. Now they can execute their plan with confidence. Also, they must cut their losses short and let the profits run.

Rajas Guna in markets or short-term trading is not bad, provided it is done in moderation, backed by strong Vidya or knowledge of technical analysis, or done after it is backed by expert advice. In order to capitalise on one's Rajasic traits, one must learn the art of technical analysis.

What is technical analysis?

Technical analysis is a technique that helps traders identify short term opportunities in the markets. It is based on the assumption that all information that can affect the performance of equity, i.e. company fundamentals, economic factors and market sentiments, is reflected already in its prices. It is based on the idea that prices are determined by the interaction of supply and demand. Price and volume reflect the collective behaviour of buyers and sellers. The approach of technical analysts is to forecast the direction of prices through the study of patterns in historical market data expressed as the price of a stock and volume of trade.

Price is the end result of the battle between the forces of supply and demand for the company's stock. Let's try and understand why the price of a stock goes up. It is simple, more buyers (demand) than sellers (supply). After all, the value exists for any asset only when someone is willing to pay for it.

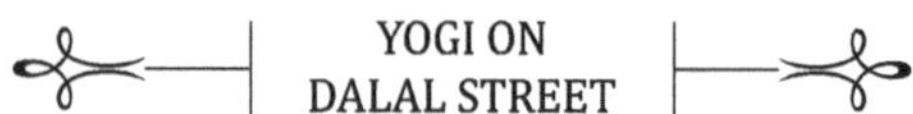

Technical analysis is a method of evaluating securities by analysing the statistics generated by market activity. It is based on three assumptions:

1. The market discounts everything
2. Prices move in trends
3. History tends to repeat itself

Technical analysis relies on the assumption that the market discounts everything in the stock's current price, be it hope or fear and knowledge, including future expectations. The buyers generate demand for the stock and the sellers create its supply. Whatever reasons prompt a buyer to buy and a seller to sell get represented in the price that the buyer pays for the stock and the seller gets for it.

The market moves in 'trends' each and every time the price moves in a certain direction. For example, in up trending markets, market participants get greedy and want to buy, irrespective of the high price. Likewise in a down trend, market participants want to sell irrespective of the low and unattractive prices.

Technical analysis also assumes that history repeats itself. This happens because market participants consistently react to price movements in a remarkably similar way. Any trading method or system that works well on a broad sample of historical data may have validity when applied to future trading environments. This assumption arises from the fact that human psychology does not change. The psychology that drives the price upward in the bull market will be seen over and over again in subsequent bull markets as well. The same is the case with bear markets.

Trend, an important concept in technical analysis, is but the general direction in which a security or market is headed.

Types of Trend

- Up Trend: A market is said to be in an uptrend if prices are consistently reaching higher highs and retracing in higher lows.

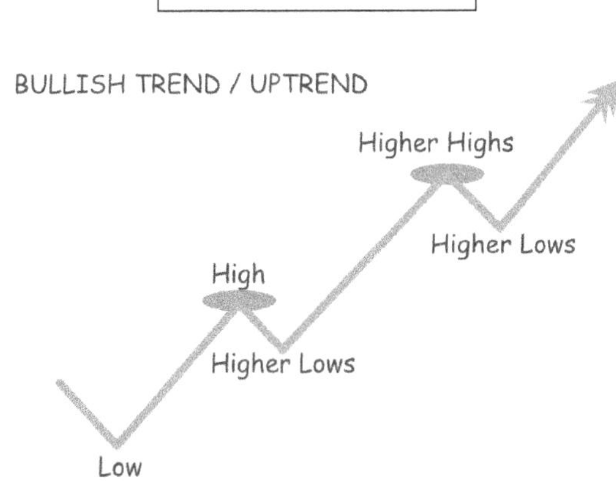

- Downtrend: A market is in a downtrend if prices are consistently declining to lower lows and retracing to lower highs.

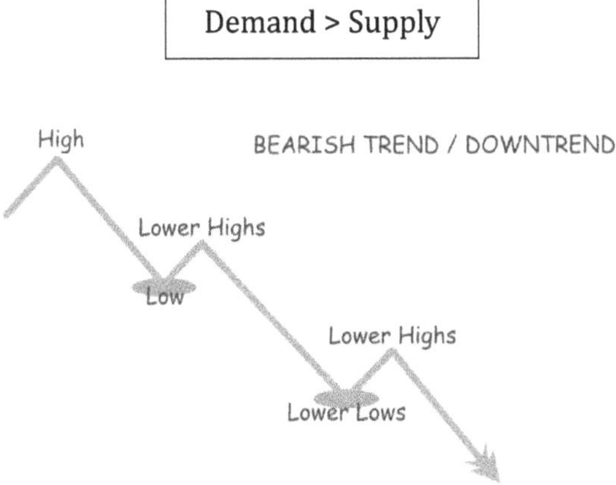

Sideways Trend: A market is in a sideways trend when demand and supply are equal. Due to this, prices remain range bound.

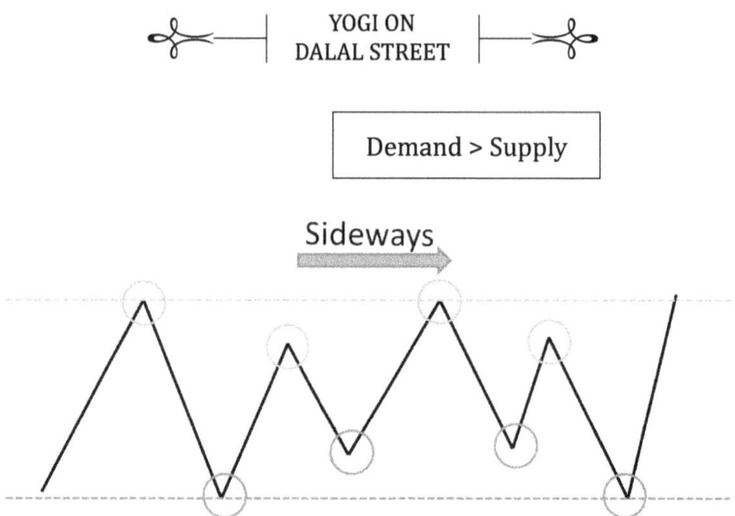

Role of Volume: It is also important to find out the strength of price movement through volume. Volume is simply the number of shares that trade over a given period of time. Volume is an important aspect of technical analysis because it is used to confirm the trend. Higher volumes indicate that the stock is more active and vice versa. Any price movement, up or down, with relatively high volume is seen as a stronger, more relevant move than a similar move with weak volume. Therefore, if one is looking at a large price movement, one should also examine the volume to see whether it tells the same story.

Role of a Trend Line: Drawing a trend line by connecting prices can enable us to identify if a trend is continuing or in reversal. In an uptrend, a trend line connects the increasing lows in the price, whereas, in a downtrend a similar line can be drawn to connect the decreasing highs in the price. This is depicted using **Charts**.

A chart is a simple graphical representation of a series of prices over a set time frame.

Since technical analysis involves a study of the movement in share prices, a number of charts can be used to analyze the historical trend in these prices and where this trend is expected to head in future.

There are different types of charts viz., line chart, candlestick chart, point & figure chart, bar chart, etc., which are used for Technical Analysis. Candlestick is the most popularly used chart.

Imbalances in supply and demand that are reflected by strong movements away from the trend line, create support and resistance levels.

- **Support Level**: When an overwhelmingly high number of buyers (demand) step into a stock which has been declining since the past few trading sessions, the stock has reached a level of support. At this level, buying is expected to emerge and it prevents further price decreases.
- **Resistance Level**: On the other hand, a large number of sellers (supply) might prevent a stock which has been moving higher over the past few trading sessions from further increase, by selling it. At this level, called the resistance level, selling is expected to emerge and it prevents further price rises.

A chart indicating such support and resistance levels can be seen below:

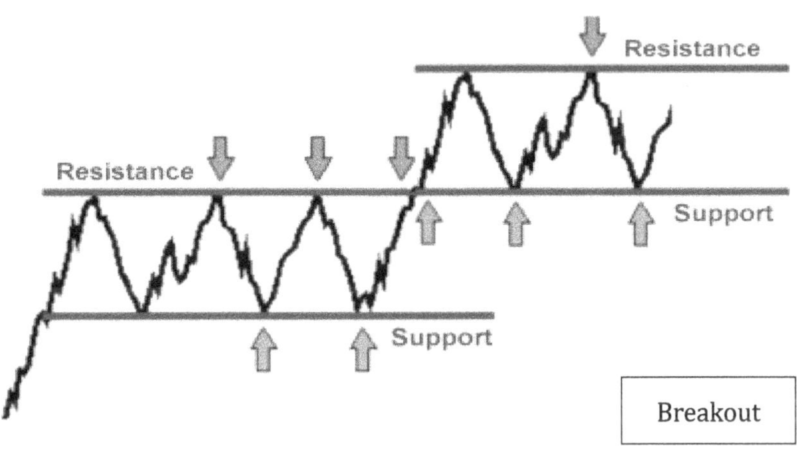

Note that support and resistance levels often switch their zones. When the price crosses the trend line by a significant amount along with a high volume, say, it beats its resistance level, a breakout occurs. Similarly, if it beats its support level, a breakdown is said to occur. After a breakout, the price point which earlier served as a resistance level in an uptrend, due to high selling, becomes a support level for a downtrend and vice versa. This concept is called a **change in polarity**.

One should also remember the following four aspects while doing technical analysis:

a. **Trades/ Bets** – Technical Analysis is used to identify short term trades. Long term investment opportunities are better identified using fundamental analysis.

b. **Risk** – Technical analysis involves risk as one expects returns over a short period of time. It can happen that in the case of an adverse movement in the stock, the trades one has entered into start making a loss. Usually, in such situations, traders hold on to their loss, hoping they can recover the loss. However, it is very important to cut the losses by setting a stop loss and moving on to identify another opportunity.

c. **Return** – As Technical analysis based trades are short-term in nature, one should not expect huge returns within a short duration of time. Instead, one should identify frequent short term trading opportunities, which can give one small but consistent profits.

d. **Holding Period/ Duration** – Technical analysis based trades can end on the same day (intraday) or last for a few days or weeks (positional). It is very important to keep in mind the risk-return relationship while holding a stock for a certain period.

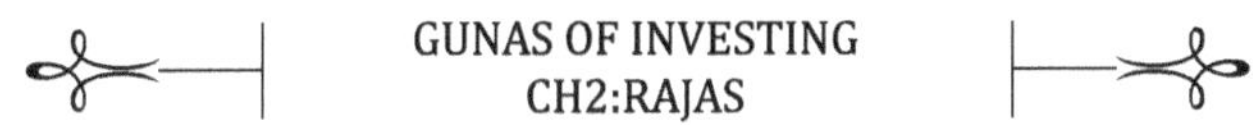

Technical analysis integrates prices, volumes and duration into price charts, points of support and resistance in charts and price trends. By observing price and volume patterns, technical analysts try to understand if there is an adequate buying interest that may take prices up, or vice versa.

These are the basic concepts of Technical Analysis. One can pick any dedicated book on Technical Analysis for in-depth knowledge.

Channelising Rajas

Rajas and Tamas usually follow each other. Rajas bring about the over expression of energy, which eventually leads to exhaustion, in which Tamas prevails. For example, too much spicy food and alcohol are initially Rajasic or stimulating. These eventually lead to Tamasic conditions, as fatigue and plummeting of energy levels follow. Similarly, in equity markets, many short-term small gains excite a trader and one big loss creates an extremely unpleasant experience and turns one Tamasic.

In order to attain a state of Sattva or harmony, one has to master the art of channelising one's Rajasic energy and utilise it to derive maximum benefit from one's investments.

Following are the three must-have traits to be a successful trader

1. Discipline is vital

As an active participant in the markets there will be times when one feels the need to act on one's intuitions and not follow the plan they had initially laid out, because they think "this time it is different" and "I will only do it once", etc. Well, unfortunately it doesn't work that way. This is how most traders end up losing money. One should be proactive in knowing every possible move ahead of time and not just react to what the market gives them. One cannot afford to break rules; not even once!

2. Losing is a part of trading

Trading is a game of statistics, and as such, nothing is 100% foolproof. One will have losses; every trader does. What separates the highly successful traders from the perennial losing trader is how they lose. Learning from such mistakes is equivalent to paying a 'tuition fee' – though costly, it will help prevent us from making much bigger losses in the future. We must maintain a diligent record of all our trades, be it gains or losses, to improve our odds of successes in the future.

3. Define a time horizon and stick to it

Arguably the most important trait of the world's greatest traders is the ability to set out with and stick to a clear and executable strategy. Before entering into a trade, one should be sure whether it is for a day, week or month.

Conclusion

Summing it up, the Rajasic trait brings unlimited energy along, but it only helps if channelised properly. If one has a trader's mindset, their Rajasic side predominates, and if it goes out of hand, their activity in the market could lead to a string of losses for a series of trades. Hence, it is a must for traders to keep control over their energies, learn technical analysis and use it religiously to properly channelise their Rajasic energies. Backed by technical knowledge, traders have higher chances of making successful trades. In case one makes losses while trading, it should be taken up in a sporting spirit. The temptation in such cases is to approach the market with a vengeance to make good all the losses. This should be avoided. In such a situation it makes sense to use discrimination or Viveka and let the Rajasic fervour subside and make way for Tamas or inactivity. During the period of rest, one should think about what caused the losses. Once one feels rested and the storm of Rajas subsides, one must approach the market, armed with the insights gained during the period of rest. One should write down the steps one intends to take to avoid making the same mistakes again.

Chapter 3

Sattva

SATTVA

तत्रसत्वंनिर्मलत्वात्प्रकाशकमनामयम् |

सुखसङ्गेनबध्नातिज्ञानसङ्गेनचानघ || 6 ||

Tatra Sattvaṁ nirmalatvāt prakāśhakam anāmayam

sukha-saṅgena badhnāti jñāna-saṅgena chānagha

O sinless one, it binds the soul by creating attachment for a sense of happiness and knowledge.

– 14.6 Bhagavad Gita

The Yoga Sutra urges seekers to rise above the lethargy of Tamas and the excitability of Rajas and become more Sattvic. This goal is achieved through careful regulation of diet, lifestyle, thinking, emoting and speaking. A Yogi eats Sattvic foods, keeps the company of Sattvic people, lives a Sattvic life and earns a living from means that are Sattvic. For a Yogi, the Sattvic state enables the mind to become clear and transparent, like a mirror. Such a mind reflects the world accurately without any distortion and when it is turned within, it beholds the soul that is animating the body, mind, intellect and the ego. The clarity that Sattva brings makes it the most desirable Guna for an investor. Individuals in

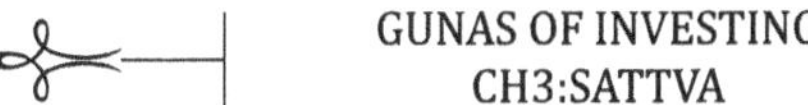

whom this Guna dominates invest across various asset classes based on their goals and risk profiles. They realise that equity as an asset class has the potential to provide multi-fold returns provided one invests for the long-term backed by Vidya either researched on one's own or provided by reputed research experts. Such Sattvic investors keep Rajas in check by refraining from needlessly churning their portfolio or taking too many risks in the short-term. They rely on stocks with strong fundamental and structural stories and do not get too bothered with short-term ups or downs. They do not overly rely on any particular asset class and build a well-diversified portfolio through asset allocation.

Investors in whom the Sattva Guna predominates always make long-term investments after performing thorough due diligence. Having developed conviction about the soundness of the investment, they monitor the developments strictly with objectivity. They do not get carried away with the noise around and take actions only after they have analysed the impact of the development on the future of the investment. They do not get perturbed by volatility in the market and use it to their advantage by accumulating at lower prices, whenever an opportunity arises. An investor who operates from a space of Sattva focuses on a handful of opportunities, employing their attention on stories that make strong business sense. They develop a well-diversified but a concentrated portfolio that gives them good returns over a period of time along with peace of mind. Having an objective attitude towards everything, the Sattva Guna Sampann (rich in the quality of Sattva) investor is in a position to enjoy every aspect of life without a tinge of worry due to frivolous developments that cause market volatility.

Fundamental Analysis

An accomplished Sattva Guna investor uses fundamental analysis to weigh the worth of tradable securities, be it equity instruments or debt or a hybrid of the two as a potential investment.

Analysing a security (or an investment opportunity) involves studying the historical and projected data of a company from an investment point of view. When one makes an investment, one expects a certain target return on the investment after a specific time period, be it one year, five years or even a decade. The return one earns may be periodic, like an annual dividend, or a capital gain earned when the stock is sold at the end of the period for which the investment has been made. Intelligent investing involves understanding and predicting the future value of a security so that by buying it at a lower value today, the investor can make money by holding it for a specific period of time.

A security is said to be a worthy investment if the current price of the security is at a discount to the cumulative present value of the future cash flows accruing out of the business.

Now, one has to decide what should be paid for the returns to be received at the end of the specified period. These periodic returns can be fixed (as in the fixed income investment) or can be variable (as in equity investments). Unlike buying a consumable item, buying an investment does not immediately give a feel of the value that one receives.

Buying the right stocks at the right time is difficult. But deciding when to sell is even tougher. Fundamental analysis gives one a better understanding of such value traps to look out for when it comes to making decisions.

The chief idea is to buy excellent businesses at a price that makes business sense. This means that money invested in a business will offer the investor the highest predictable annual compounding rate of return with the least amount of risk. This can be achieved if the investor stays invested for the long term.

There are two approaches to investing using fundamental analysis, as mentioned earlier. Top-down and bottom-up investing. The objective of both is to identify fundamentally strong stocks. The top-down investing approach involves analysing the big picture, i.e., the economy, and understanding the characteristics of the industry and then boiling it down to companies within that industry/ sector. A bottom-up investor starts by analysing the individual attributes of the company based on fundamentals and as long as the story is intact, the business cycle or broader industry conditions are secondary or of less concern. In both cases, analysing fundamentally is a must.

Fundamental analysis includes Economy, Industry and Company analysis (EIC analysis), where all the qualitative and quantitative aspects are considered and the attractiveness of the investment proposition of the industry/ company is determined.

Economic analysis

Economic analysis factors in insights from microeconomics as well as macroeconomics. Microeconomics is the study of economics from the perspective of a single economic unit like a consumer, a business or a retail enterprise.

Macroeconomics takes a bird-eye view of an economic system and portrays the overall economy, like the nation's growth and government policies. Microeconomics is the study of the behaviour and decisions of individuals and businesses; how it affects the supply and demand for goods and services, which in turn signals

where the economy has to direct its productive activities. Consumer demand drives the prices and the production levels of goods and services in an economy.

Macroeconomics helps us understand the general state of the economy. It monitors and evaluates the health of the overall economy on the basis of parameters like domestic production, domestic consumption, general price levels, growth and quality of life. Macroeconomics helps us understand drivers of income, savings, investments and employment in an economy. Macroeconomic models help governments and central bankers formulate economic policies for achieving long-run economic growth with stability. It also helps us understand various aspects of international trade of goods and services like exports, imports, balance of payments, exchange rate dynamics, etc. It facilitates an understanding of how inter-linkages across economies work.

Stages of an economic cycle or business cycle

Countries go through economic cycles. The stage at which the country is, directly impacts industry as well as individual companies. It affects investment decisions, demand, employment and the profitability of companies.

Certain products, where customers cannot postpone their purchase decisions, are not affected by economic cycles. The upward and downward fluctuations of a country are reflected in numbers relating to production, employment, investment and prices.

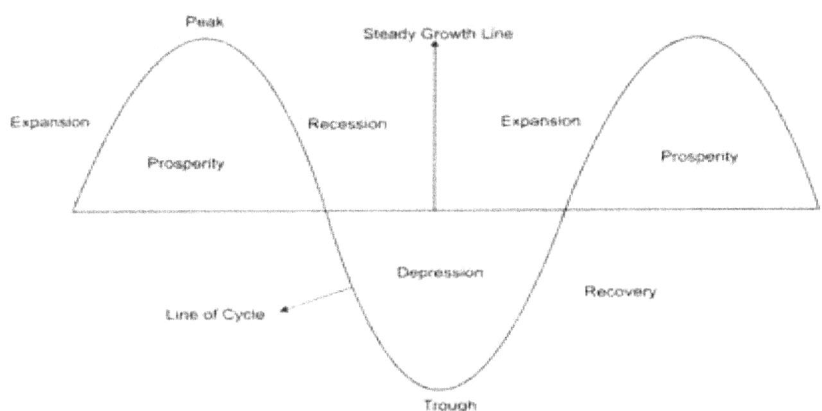

Figure-2: Representation of Phases of a Business Cycle

The two main phases in a business cycle are prosperity and depression. The cycle can be divided into expansion, peak, recession, trough and recovery.

Economies move in and out of economic expansionary and contractionary phases, which mainly depend on the demand and supply scenario. The Indian economy is in an expansionary mode; it is at the same stage where the US economy was in the 1980s and China was in the 1990s. We very well know how these two economies have fared over the next two decades. As these economies expanded, consumption-led demand created opportunities for many businesses to prosper. As the economies grew, the earnings of various segments of society improved, their consumption pattern changed with increased focus on discretionary spends. The demand for automobiles, consumer durables, FMCG, electrical and electronic goods, media, clothing and home textiles etc rose. People spent on travel and tourism, education, entertainment, insurance, along with investments. The mode of investments shifted from physical goods, like gold and real estate, to financial assets like equities, electronic formats of gold etc. Thus, the way of living gave way to the new sunrise sectors.

Smart investors often identify these sunrise sectors and create wealth by investing at their infancy and holding on to them through their growth / development phase. A common investor can benefit from the rising demand by investing in the maturity phase of the business even if they cannot invest at the infancy of the business.

As every economy goes through business cycles, an investor has to position an investment taking cognizance of the state of the economy, its position on the economic cycle curve along with its prospects, after undertaking a thorough study of economic and industrial analysis. Let us understand the concept of fundamental analysis, using an example from a small industry within the ~$67bn Indian Auto ancillary industry.

The industry being referred to here is the **Indian Steel Wheels industry** whose market size is ~$0.95bn. This industry involves manufacturing of wheels for passenger vehicles (PV), commercial vehicles (CV), 2 & 3 wheelers, tractors, and Off the Road vehicles. It is important to understand the players within the industry, their market shares, Compounded Annual Growth Rate (CAGR) in the wheels industry in the last 5–10 years, triggers for the auto ancillary and, consequently, the auto industry going forward and export opportunities in this space.

The proximity of the wheel manufacturing plants to the plants of Original Equipment Manufacturers (OEMs) helps in controlling the logistics cost and timely sourcing of raw material for the producer as well for the OEMs.

Let us look at the industry through the lens of the factors for industry analysis:

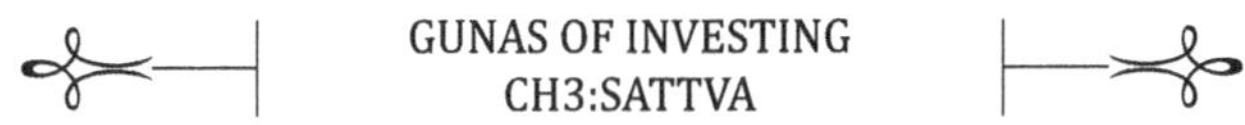

Number of Competitors: Steel wheel industry is duopolistic (only two players) and the country lacks dependable sources of Quality Alloy wheel makers. Indian firms are collaborating with foreign companies to produce quality alloy wheels.

Product Differentiation: All auto segments, except PV and motorcycles, use only steel wheels; only ultra high end motorcycles (which is currently a very small segment) employ alloy wheels. Alloy wheels share in PV is 24%, growing at 20% CAGR as OEMs have started adapting to the changing trend given the finish and aesthetic looks that alloy wheels bring about.

Number of Suppliers: Steel and aluminium are raw materials for steel wheel making. There are a large number of steel and aluminium alloy suppliers. Wheel making companies have their own supply chain set to meet their raw material requirements which saves on cost.

Entry Barriers: Auto Industries are concentrated in certain geographical clusters like Chennai, Pune, Sanand, Gurugram etc. For a new player to enter the market, they would have to set up their plants near or within these clusters. Initial investment, incubation period for getting certified by the OEMs, long gestation period due to high rejection rate before stabilization of production process, technological know-how, etc. are few of the entry barriers in this business. Foreign firms with technological know-how are increasing their footprint in India using the Joint Venture route.

Switching Cost: Since wheels form an essential component of a car, they cannot be done away with. There is a high demand from car manufacturers. Since wheel making is a capital intensive process, it makes sense for OEMs to outsource their wheel requirements to specialized players instead of producing them on their own. Wheels,

being an important part, both in terms of function and looks, have stringent quality requirements making OEMs into sticky customers for the wheel suppliers.

External Environment: It is also important to understand the impact of migrations happening in the Indian Automobile industry like the advent of electric vehicles. However, in this case, a wheel which is the 'mobile' component of the car faces no threat of substitutes and will continue to be an integral component of a moving car.

After we have identified a strong industry on the basis of our previous analysis, we would now move forward to analyze the companies in the industry and select the best from the lot to invest in. The analysis to be done comprises of primarily 2 aspects:

a. Qualitative Analysis
b. Quantitative Analysis

Qualitative Analysis involves identifying the following factors in a company:

Strengths and Weaknesses: These are internal to the company. Individual strengths help create a moat around the company to protect it from predatory moves by competition. These factors differentiate the company from its competitors and help it protect its margins. These strengths can be in the form of a long association with OEMs, technological lead, backward integration etc. For an alloy wheel maker, its first mover advantage by establishing the production process, regular supply of quality products right on time as required by the OEM could be the strength. In contrast, weaknesses can make a company vulnerable to competition.

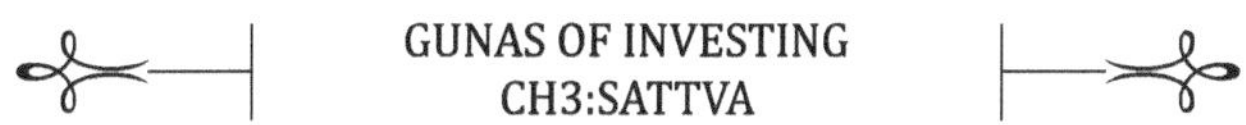

Opportunities and Threats: They deal with the external environment of the company. The company needs to identify opportunities at the earliest and gain the first mover advantage in the same so as to get ahead of competition. Threats can have a strong detrimental impact on the functioning of a business and thus a strategy to combat these should be devised well in advance.

Market Share: A company with a high market share commands pricing power and might also have monopoly over the industry. It cannot be easily dislodged by fringe players in the industry.

Growth Potential: A company with a niche product, a strong ability to identify opportunities and favourable industrial factors will have a strong growth potential. In the long run, it is these companies which would give maximum returns to its shareholders.

Quantitative Analysis involves analyzing the financial statements of the company, i.e. Balance Sheets, Profit and Loss Statement and Cash Flow Statement and drawing inferences from the same. This will be covered in detail in a later part of this book.

It is also necessary to understand the target OEMs which the company is catering to, and check if it has any client concentration risk. It is important to understand the volume and the revenue mix of wheels of PVs, CVs, 2&3 wheelers, tractors etc. The capacity set up for wheels manufacturing and the capacity utilization rates needs to be tracked. The capital expenditure plans of the company for setting up additional capacity for expansion or for strategic cost reduction initiatives needs to be understood. Here, management guidance holds a lot of importance to understand the future expansion plans for the company. Additionally, it is worthwhile to know if the company is entering into forward integration (purchase or control of distributors) or backward integration (purchase or control of suppliers) to save on cost.

As we mentioned about the migrations in this industry, one more shift that is being observed is from steel wheels to alloy wheels in passenger vehicles. Thus, we also need to check whether wheel making companies are adapting to the changing trend and setting up capacities for manufacturing of alloy wheels.

Therefore, the favorable economic tailwinds, leading to a rising disposable income and hence more demand for discretionary spends like automobiles, make this industry an attractive sector for investments. Again, within this sector, automobile ancillary companies like wheel manufacturing companies with competitive advantage and growth visibility can be looked into as an investment avenue post thorough due diligence.

Harnessing Sattva

As the internal state where Sattva predominates is the most preferred for an investor, let's take a look at the essential traits that one must have in order to be rooted to the Sattva Guna:

1. **Filter out market noise:** Commit investment only after thorough due diligence. Once the investment is done, one must keep oneself insulated from market chatter. Fundamentally strong stocks would bounce back in case of market correction due to extraneous factors. Hence, one should cut oneself from the noise and stay focussed on the fundamentals.

2. **Be patient:** Equity investments bear fruit in the long run. Patience always pays; one should stay invested for the long term.

3. **Do things differently:** Be greedy when the world is fearful and be fearful when the world is greedy. A Yogic investor would never follow the herd and would make decisions backed by fundamentals in the business.

4. **Resist the temptation to speculate:** Keep away from speculation, it always drains both money and energy.

5. **Never stop learning:** Be open to learn; knowledge is the key to success. Albert Einstein had well said," Wisdom is not a product of schooling but of the lifelong attempt to acquire it."

Sattva is not an easy state to be in at all times. It requires patience, a great deal of humility and knowledge of one's own limitations. Sattvic investors constantly challenge their own theories and try to learn from other people's wisdom and experience.

Conclusion

Every personality is made of three Gunas, and at any particular time one of the three dominates the other two. For a healthy personality, the harmonious blend of all these three traits is essential. Say after playing a football game, which calls for the Rajasic side of the personality, one must rest, which is a Tamasic state. One also has to calmly contemplate or analyze the game and evaluate one's performance dispassionately. Such contemplation is Sattvic.

An investment portfolio should ideally have proper representation of all three Gunas. Fixed-deposits along with real estate and gold (if one is interested) represents the Tamasic Guna offering liquidity on tap, if required, in case of an emergency. A dynamic trading portfolio with a high churn ratio containing equities and derivatives represents the Rajasic Guna. This portfolio offers reasonably good returns in the short-term. A long-term portfolio signifying the Sattvic Guna would comprise a proper blend of long-term equity investments giving multiple returns over the years.

The proportions of these three classes are to be decided by the investor on one's own, based on the risk profile and understanding of different asset classes.

Module 4

Vrittis of Investing

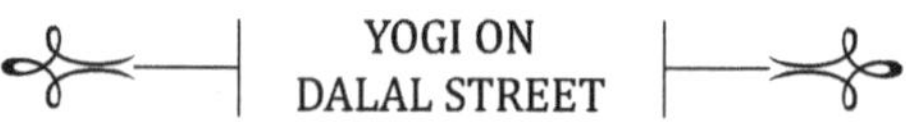

Preface

The concept of Vritti is central to the main definition of Yoga

योगश्चित्तवृत्तिनिरोधः

Yogash Chitta Vritti Nirodhah

Yoga is the process of quieting of the constantly shifting states of mind

– 1.2 Patanjali Yoga Sutra

Weakening the hold of emotions on the mind is an important goal of Yoga. Freed from emotional experience, the thinking of a Yogic investor becomes increasingly rational. It is not difficult to see how a stable mind can help an investor navigate the equity market with clarity.

Investing is not just a game of numbers; it is application of the mind to see through the numbers. Yoga, which helps to calm one's mind and invigorate the body, has complete solutions for investors who fail to apply their mind. 'Chitta', in Yoga, comprises the part of the human consciousness and mind-field that reflects the world. It is that likeness or reflection of the object in the Chitta that makes knowledge and comprehension possible. Chitta is unstable by nature. It is affected not just by what it observes in the world but also by memories that evoke strong emotions. The mind is drawn to objects that evoke pleasant memories. And it is repulsed by objects that evoke painful memories. Like children who fashion animals out of playing clay, and restore it to its old form as a lump of clay when they are done playing, Chitta assumes the shapes of things it beholds. This tendency of the mind to mime or reflect what it observes has been called Vritti in the Yoga Sutra. Vrittis arise not just when objects are observed, they also arise when an object is contemplated or

remembered. Memory is not just data; as mentioned earlier it is also a storehouse of powerful emotions. These emotional memories influence, refract and distort everything they behold.

A stable Chitta that manages to reflect the world faithfully without distorting its true nature is central to the art of investing. We are the sum total of our experience and since our experience forms all perceptions, analysis and decisions, the choices we believe to be 'rational' may not be rational at all. Experience colours and distorts everything.

It is this innate nature of Chitta with its ever shifting Vrittis that helps investors who are data-driven to win in a market driven by strong emotions. Emotions mislead. Hard data is a more reliable pointer towards truth.

Sutra 1.3 says, "tada drashtuh svarupe-vasthanam" meaning "At that moment, truth of pure nature remains (self-realization)." Only when the mind is no longer in turmoil, that the true awareness surfaces. In reality, however, the mind is almost always preoccupied and it loses its self-awareness.

Sutra 1.4 says, "Vritti sarupyam itaratra" meaning "At other times Vritti shifts/assumes shapes according to objects it beholds and identifies with." The expression 'other times' refers to the state of ordinary consciousness, which is contrasted with the Chitta of the enlightened soul, which is described in the Sutra that precedes the one quoted above (Sutra 1.3).

An enlightened soul, a Siddha Yogi, reaches a stage where the Vrittis in the Chitta or the mind are completely reined in or calmed. Nothing disturbs such a Yogi as long as they are in that supreme state. Even a moment in that supreme state changes the Chitta forever. For such a Siddha, even mundane worldly activities like investing take on a clarity that can only be imagined by those in ordinary states of consciousness. This happens because the mind becomes supremely rational and also because Sidhhi or success in Yoga awakens intuition. A rational mind that remains unswayed when the whole world is in an emotional turmoil and an awakened intuition are the biggest weapons in the arsenal of a Yoga investor.

Sutra 1.5 delves more into the Vrittis when it states "vrittayah panchatayyah klishtAklishtah" meaning there are five overall categories of fluctuations (Vrittis) in the field of the mind. Before we delve into what Vrittis mean and how they affect an investor, one must note that these Vrittis are either harmful/coloured by Kleshas (Klishta) or beneficial/uncoloured by Kleshas (Aklishta). For example, they can either help cultivate complete ignorance (influenced by Avidya) or consciousness (bereft of Avidya). All the five Kleshas have their influence on Vrittis. Anything at extreme ends (either beneficial or harmful) is undesirable. The coloured/ influenced versions of Vrittis are considered harmful in nature as they form an obstacle thereby blocking one's mind from seeking knowledge and using one's Viveka in application of the same. The endeavour should be to come out of a harmful shade of Vritti to a beneficial one and then move beyond it.

To delve into the concept of Klishta and Aklishta with more clarity, let us consider the example of knowledge. When can knowledge be harmful or beneficial for one? If knowledge is utilized in a sensible way, to perpetuate good, it is in its beneficial or Aklishta form. Suppose we know that it is raining quite heavily outside, we would probably call our near and dear ones and ask them if they are safe and advise them not to go outside. This is a beneficial (Aklishta) use of knowledge. On the other hand, if taxi drivers gain the same knowledge that it is raining heavily outside, they may in turn hike their fares and make it expensive for people to hail a cab. This would be a harmful or Klishta use of knowledge. The same can be studied in the case of financial markets. Gaining knowledge about the strong fundamentals and growth prospects of a company may encourage an investor to invest in that particular stock and advise friends to do so too. This would be beneficial or Aklishta use of knowledge. In contrast, if the same knowledge is used for the purpose of insider trading, one would be using knowledge harmfully or in its Klishta form.

Finally Sutra 1.6 defines these Vrittis as "Pramana Viparyaya Vikalpa Nidra smritayah". According to Patanjali's Yoga Sutra, following are the five fluctuations or modifications of mind:

1. *Pramana* (Right knowledge)
2. *Viparyaya* (Wrong knowledge)
3. *Vikalpa* (Imagination)
4. *Nidra* (Sleep)
5. *Smriti* (Memory)

Let us dwell at some length on each of the five Vrittis:

Pramana is the right knowledge, backed by proof of firsthand experience that has been validated. In investment parlance, this is primary research gathered through first hand experience with our five senses. Knowledge gathered from a visit to a supermarket to check which FMCG products are moving fast would qualify as paramana. To offer another example, this time from everyday life, with our five senses, we can say that we know what water is, because we have experienced it by touching it and using it to quench our thirst or to clean ourselves. We know the knowledge of water is valid because it is revealed to be water based on our experiences and its reality can be experienced practically. So Patanjali says that

in order for knowledge to be valid it needs to be perceived not only by the five senses, but it also needs to be experienced in practice. According to Yoga, the proper means of knowledge must rely on these three Pramanas:

Pratyakṣa — direct perception

Anumāna — inference

Agamah — testimony/word of reliable experts

Pramana is largely on the Aklishta or beneficial side. However, if one has fixed beliefs or dogmas or preconceived notions or prejudices that one clings to, which reinforce false identification and ignorance, it can be Klishta or harmful. For example, people believed the world to be flat, based on Pratyaksha (direct perception) that the horizon was flat, followed by Anumana or inference that the earth was flat, which was confirmed by the then ruling ideologies or Agamah (testimony).

Viparyaya is incorrect cognition or misconceived knowledge. Misconception is therefore a false notion based on the deceptive appearance of an object. We can mistake a rope for a snake at night. We may like to think that we go through life seeing things objectively but, in fact, we see the world as we want to see it. People who buy solely because the price of a stock is low may be under the influence of Viparaya. The value of a stock may be even lower than the present price, and the fall may reflect a weakening of fundamentals.

Viparyaya is largely on the Klishta or harmful side. However, there may be times that wrong knowledge may also help accidentally. For example, wrong knowledge that equity markets are unsafe would have helped investors in the year 2000 during the dot-com bubble or in 2008, during the subprime crisis, thereby preventing one from committing investments in those respective times.

Vikalpa or imagination is the creation of ideas in our minds. Vikalpa is a sort of a hallucination. Such a fantasy is called Vikalpa, the third modulation of mind or Chitta. Vikalpa can be of two types. One could be a joyful, pleasurable fantasy (Aklishta or beneficial side) and the other could be a nightmare that evokes fear (Klishta or harmful side). "What will happen if I die tomorrow? What if I have an accident?" These are all just simple sounds which have no value but are baseless fears in the mind. We actually can convince ourselves of a truth when in fact it is not true at all! Other translations of Vikalpa are: doubt, indecision, daydreaming. If retail investors who have just recently initiated investing in the stock markets start imagining themselves owning a private island serviced by a staff of 150, they are experiencing Vikalpa. In contrast, a billionaire who continuously stays in fear and cooks up nightmares of becoming a penniless beggar, is experiencing Vikalpa too.

Nidra is a state of deep dreamless sleep. It is the Vritti or modification or state of mind when no objects are presented to the Chitta. As a result the mind/ Chitta rests in the Vritti or state where no other Vritti can arise. It is a state where nothing that exists around the person is reflected in the Chitta. In the Yoga Sutras, Patanjali says that "deep sleep is when the mind is overcome by heaviness". When the mind is not in the first three Vrittis (valid cognition, misconception and imagination), then it goes to sleep. If one sleeps for the right amount of time it rejuvenates the body (Aklishta or beneficial side) and if one undersleeps or oversleeps, one feels drowsy or lethargic (Klishta or harmful side).

From the point of view of investment, the mind enters a state of rest. Being in Nidra for the right amount of time is important for one's investments. Staying invested in a stock without paying heed to the company's poor performance or any regulatory changes affecting the stock is harmful to the portfolio. However, at the same time, continuously churning one's portfolio is also not healthy for one's investments.

Smriti is the mental retention of a conscious experience. On the most obvious level, memories can bring one pleasure (Aklishta or beneficial side) or leave one angry, sad or agitated (Klishta or harmful side). But on a deeper level, memory influences the present situation more than one realises it. We may hold onto some painful memories which prevent us from letting go and in a way, our memories can 'steal our present moment'. By holding onto certain impressions, this can prevent us from experiencing the 'now', without bias, judgement or criticism.

Smriti, as pointed out at the beginning of the chapter, has an emotional strand that keeps one from making purely rational decisions. The emotional content in memory tends to sway investors to act under the influence of 'market sentiment'. This is why experience is not just a teacher, it is also a misleader. Memory informs as well as distorts what is before us.

Step by step approach to rein-in Vrittis

The goal of Yoga is to still or silence the modifications or Vrittis in Chitta or the mind. The goal of Yoga is to rein in Vrittis; so that when they are calm we start seeing things for what they truly are. This is easier said than done. One has to first identify the Klishta side Vritti, work upon finding a solution to convert it into the Aklishta form of the same and then silence/ calm the Vritti. Let us take an example of Raga-Dvesha. These are extreme emotions- attachment and aversions. Investors may have aversion towards equity investments due to their prior experience of losses made by themself or anybody near/ dear to them. Admitting the fact that it is unwise to avoid equity when only equity has historically generated rewarding real returns over long terms, the investor has to come to terms and take a fresh look at equity investment. One should first identify the reasons for losses made earlier. Then one has to undertake thorough due diligence on all aspects of the investment, which will eventually develop more understanding about the prospects of the intended investment or invest carefully with the help of experts. Thus, one can move from Klishta Vritti to Aklishta Vritti. Having committed to the investment, one has to practice Vairagya, thus getting bereft of both aversion and attachment towards the investment and thus allow it to grow and create wealth for one.

To summarise, an object that smells like a mango, looks like mango pulp and tastes like a mango is probably mango pulp (Pratyaksha or perception with the five senses). Alternatively, it could be artificially manufactured flavoured pulp (Viparyaya or the mistaking of the unreal for the real) that we are mistaking for mango pulp. It is also possible to pass a guava tree and imagine what it would look like laden with mangoes (Vikalpa or imagination that does not have basis in reality. A guava tree that bears mangoes is not possible). One may even be sleeping soundly when everyone else around us is enjoying mangoes (Nidra or deep sleep when one is 'dead' to the mangoes) or one may revisit the summer holidays at one's grandmother's house where one would eat juicy mangoes till one could have no more (Smriti or memory).

In our example, each Vritti has been described as a response or state of mind to the fact of mangoes. While the example of each Vritti has been explained separately, in the human mind the Vrittis act in tandem and influence each other without pause. As a mind observes the world and experiences it, not just as fact but through the spectacles of emotions, the Vrittis arise as small waves, grow in size till they turn into tsunamis and subside while another small wave awaits to create another tsunami. In a non-Yogi this process is involuntary. Yoga is the process of making one conscious of the process of rising and subsiding of Vritti, and taming them through clearly outlined techniques to the point where they can finally be transcended.

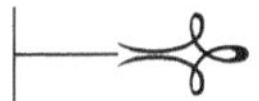

Chapter 1

Pramana

PRAMANA

प्रत्यक्षानुमानाअगमाःप्रमाणानि

Pratyaks anuman Agamah Pramanini

The different kinds of proof the mind requires are the obvious experiential proof, inferential proof and trustworthy testimony or scriptural proof.

– 1.7 Patanjali Yoga Sutra

Pramana means knowledge validated by 'proof'. We must understand that it is experience or anubhava through which we acquire knowledge about anything.

Pramana has two important aspects. Firstly, for any knowledge to be considered as Pramana, it has to be about something new, i.e. one has to get to know about it for the first time in one's life. In case an individual is re-reading or re-learning what one has already read/learned before, it would be considered as Smriti (memory) rather than Pramana. Secondly, Pramana can never be contradicted by anything else. This is because it is based on proof rather than hearsay.

So how is it that we acquire knowledge?

1. **Pratyaksha (Direct experience):** It involves acquiring knowledge through the direct use of our five senses i.e. smell, taste, vision, sound and touch. It is based on the philosophy that seeing is believing.

2. **Anumana (Inference):** It is our ability to apply logic and reason to figure things out for ourselves. For example, if one sees smoke coming out at a distance, one may infer that there is a fire.

3. **Agamah (Trustworthy testimony):** It stands for trusting in the knowledge and experience of someone else. For example, the fact that there are eight planets in the solar system revolving around the Sun cannot be verified by us directly. However, we do rely on the testimony of accomplished astronomers and believe what comes from them.

An ordinary man depends just on Pratyaksha for knowledge. A more evolved person uses Anumana along with Pratyaksha. A Yogi utilises all three proofs to validate knowledge.

In the context of investing, there is Pramana that the equity has given excellent returns since its inception. The index has moved from level to level over this period despite the sporadic deceleration brought about by domestic as well as global developments. The journey has been marked by different events and happenings that have shaped the course of the markets. It has also been proved beyond doubt that equities have beaten inflation over the long term to create wealth for investors. Having said that, we need to understand how to create wealth by making the right investments in equity.

Patanjali reveals that the milestones of sound knowledge are crossed on the routes of *Pratyaksha, Anumana* and *Agamah.* The one who studies the market directly, say, by visiting 100 different variants of jewellery stores covering the entire spectrum, to understand how the segment is doing, is walking the Pratyaksha mode. Pratyaksha Praman is the primary means of gaining first-hand knowledge, where we study and come to our own conclusions. The response of an audience to a movie release would be the perfect example of Praman. If the movie is liked by the audience, they will flock to the theatres. A 'Housefull' Board or a long waiting period for an advance booking and excellent critics' review are indicative of the success of the film. This is Anumana. It will then be confirmed by the collection numbers at the box-office. If the film bombs, one can conclude that it fails to attract a crowd, and the box office counters would not be ringing. This would be the Pratyaksha Pramana. An analysis of the success of the films released in a quarter would give an idea about the business of exhibition centres in that particular quarter.

If we decide to go by the advice of experts whose credibility is beyond doubt and whose research credentials are impeccable, we are following the Agamah route. The wise may, as mentioned above, choose to use all three routes, before they take a decision. In the world of equity, one must understand that behind every stock there is a company and how well one knows the company will make all the difference in one's investment judgment.

Pratyaksha (direct experience) and Anumana (inference)

The true evidence of a company's state of affairs is scripted in its Annual Reports or the Pramana. Understanding annual reports can also help one in making an informed estimate or *Anumana* of the company's future.

So, what does an annual report tell us? It is all about the hard facts and figures, duly audited by the qualified auditors and reported to the regulatory body. The Annual Report provides a summary of the company's performance in the preceding year along with a glimpse of the future. The audited numbers cannot be tinkered with unless there is some restatement due to change in policies, neither can they be doctored, though there are a few outliers in the history, e.g. Satyam Computers, Enron, WorldCom etc. These hard facts become the basis of analysing the company performance in the past.

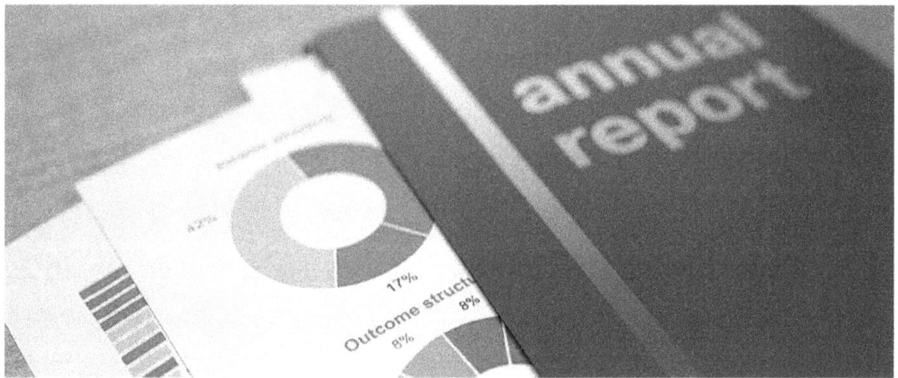

How to read Annual Reports

Annual Reports contain financial statements - both Profit & Loss accounts and the balance sheet along with cash flow statements, of the concerned year and comparisons with the previous year. Together, financial statements report the performance of a company in the concerned year in terms of the revenues generated, profits earned, capital expenditure made and the change in debt, if any, along with net cash inflows and outflows.

- The balance sheet gives an idea about the assets and liabilities of a company at any given point in time.
- The profit and loss statement depicts the profitability of a company's business.

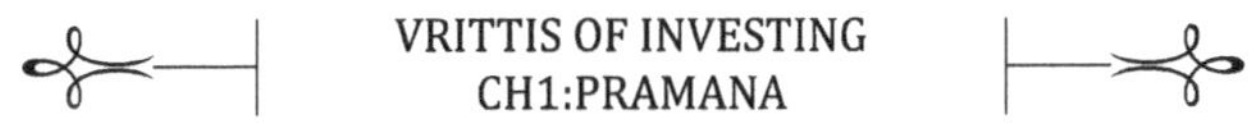

- The cash flow statements deal with the flow of cash and its deployment through operating and financing activities; it reconciles the above two financial statements (Balance Sheet and P&L) to give an idea about the sustainability of the business in the long run.

Analysing all financial statements gives a clear understanding of how the business is handled by management - do they walk the talk?

Interpreting financial statements and making Anumana (inference)

One should compare historical i.e. 5–10 years of financial statements for a company and check whether the revenues, margins and profits are growing along with the rate of growth. If the profits are seen to be growing at a rate higher than the revenues, it shows that the company has pricing power, a sustainable moat around the business and that efficient strategy has been applied by the management to prevail in the face of adversity.

Check whether the balance sheet has become stronger over these years or weakened? The balance sheet becomes stronger when the net worth improves and the debt reduces and vice-versa. Moreover, the net worth should improve due to the operational profitability of the concern and not due to fund raising by shareholders.

Verify if the business is generating cash or consuming it? The cash flow statement gives the true picture of business success. Cash generating potential differs from business to business - some industries are more cash intensive than others but no business will survive for long without generating positive cash for its shareholders. Positive cash generation means long term cash inflows exceed long term cash outflows of the company. The lesson to be taken home

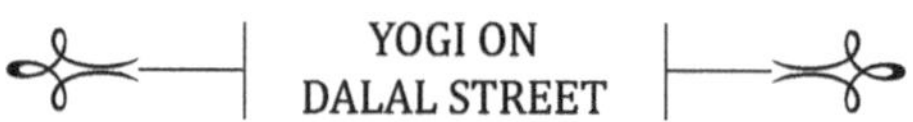

- free cash flow for the company is the king. Free cash flow is the cash thrown up by the business after taking care of all its in-house requirements. A company generating positive free cash flow would command a premium multiple while the one consuming cash will command a low multiple in the stock market. A simple thumb rule that is practiced by domestic businessmen emphasises that for every Rs 100 invested in a business, one should get Rs. 130 at the end of the year after deducting all the associated costs.

Financial statements are made for both standalone entities and consolidated ones. The consolidated financial statements contain the numbers of standalone entities consolidated with the subsidiaries. If possible one should also have a look at the individual financial statements of the subsidiaries.

Management perspective

In addition to the historical performance, Annual Reports also contain a section named Management Discussion and Analysis (MDA). In this section, the management gives an overview of the business and the industry in general and their tentative plans in near future along with different risks associated with the business. Generally, an industry overview is also discussed in the MDA, which gives a clear idea about the competitive nature of the business, technological developments, and threats, if any. If one reads the Annual Reports of the competition to the company one intends to invest in, one gets an overview of the thought processes among industry participants.

It is important to read the chairman's message in the Annual Reports to understand the vision of the person sitting at the top, their take on the year gone by and their future plans. One can also evaluate the connection of the chairman with the business. Are they transparent enough to share the roadblocks or issues faced by the company or do they just share positive developments, and dangle lofty targets before the eyes of their shareholders? The chairman's message also helps us grasp if the management team, led by the chairman, executes and implements the strategies outlined in previous Annual Reports. Through the study of the Annual Reports, one understands whether the management is willing to share the unvarnished truth with common shareholders, or maintains opacity in its dealing with minority shareholders. The chairman, being the head of the business, should own up to the failures of the business and share the successes with the team.

Dissecting trivial information

In addition to the Annual Reports, there are other reports that deal with corporate governance like energy efficiency, shareholder information, CSR report, director's report and auditor's report, etc. The notes on accounts give the breakup of the details in financial statements. The footnotes, in particular, are of prime importance. They offer a good description of the company's debt, like the term, the structure and different components. Further, additional information like off-balance sheet liabilities, contingent liabilities, operating leases, legal liabilities, future contingent liabilities or promises (maybe due to any M&A activities) etc. can also be obtained from the footnotes. Certain developments should raise red flags, say a change in message from year to year, an incorporation of liability suddenly after an event, sudden change in accounting practices, or change in auditors, etc.

Thus, the facts reported in the Annual Reports are concrete information about the company that can be utilized to construct a model to predict the future (Anumana) of the business. Different events, both domestic and global, shaped the course of a business in the past. One can further familiarise oneself with these events by reading up online and understanding the subject in greater depth. Such independent study provides the context in which one can make greater sense of the data provided by the Annual Reports. Equipped with knowledge from such vigorous study, it becomes substantially easier to get a clear picture about how a company responds to such events. One should also note the response of the share price to different events in the past.

Seeking advice from experts

Finally after seeking the desired Pratyaksha knowledge through the annual reports and deriving an inference i.e. Anumana about the future prospects of the investment idea, one should further bolster the information gathered from annual reports with more trustworthy testimony (Agamah), which is what market gurus and experts are saying about that prospective company. While market gurus may differ in opinion, it would make sense to arrive at a consensus estimate of various reputed research houses on that particular stock. This would help validate one's opinion and confidence in the potential of the concerned investments.

Conclusion

Investment decisions should be based on past behaviour and projected future performance of a stock or mutual fund, but it should not be the only reason for investment. Future growth prospects coupled with valuations would be the basic cause for appreciation of investments over the long term. In order to project the future, one has to have all the facts about the past and present (Pratyaksha), which happen to be the basic foundation of the projections (Anumana). Once convinced about an investment prospect, one must also seek views of experts (Agamah) to validate the investment idea(s). The Pratyaksha, Anumana and Agamah are the very pillars on which the castle of projections in the future rests. If the pillars are strong, so would be the castle and vice-versa. Pratyaksha testifies the hard facts, tests it against the tide of time which is then used to extend the logic to a larger sample to arrive at an Anumana. This is then cross checked from the testimonials of the learned. All these three steps are essential for one to become a Yoga investor.

Chapter 2

Viparyaya

VIPARYAYA

विपर्ययोमिथ्याज्ञानमतद्रूपप्रतिष्ठम्

Viparyayo mithyā-jñānam-atadrūpa pratiṣṭham

Viparyaya or Illusion is false knowledge formed of a thing other than what it is.

– 1.8 Patanjali Yoga Sutra

Misconceptions and wrong notions cloud the opinion of an individual from time to time in life. It is not easy to look at a thing as it is and in its correct form and feature. There is always a propensity to inaccurately perceive an object, because our mind interprets or projects information wrongly. Just as a house is to be built upon a good, solid foundation, our ideas and opinions should also be based on relevant and correct facts in order to be considered valid. However, this is not always so.

Viparyaya can be also termed as "bias" in perceiving something to be other than what it really is. The Klishta side of Viparyaya leads to forming an opinion by looking at things as we want to perceive it i.e. one becomes judgemental or applies filters to perceive things. Viparyaya or bias in perception is largely Klishta or on the harmful side. Aklishta, the beneficial side of Viparyaya, can be beneficial accidentally only. An old adage goes, "Ignorance is bliss". Therefore, sometimes people who are ill-informed about equity are better off staying away from markets as they tend to buy recklessly based on hearsay or rumours. Viparyaya is more often than not due to Avidya (ignorance) which makes equity market participants suffer from 'n' number of prejudices. It engulfs logical thought processes and pushes it towards irrationality.

We are often deceived by our senses. While it is said that seeing is believing, there is such a thing as a mirage. A mirage deceives people into believing that there is water at a distance. However, the water seen in a mirage does not actually exist. While, experientially, the perception is real, the outcome of chasing a mirage is frustrating failure. Therefore, in certain situations what one perceives is not necessarily a true representation of reality. This is not to say that there is something wrong with one's senses, but rather that one's mind has a tendency to introduce Viparyaya or biases in processing certain kinds of information and events.

Let us understand some Viparyaya (biases) of an investor which lead to misconception in the equity markets:

The need to confirm

We like to think that if we carefully gather and evaluate facts and data before coming to an investment decision, we cannot go wrong. But the picture of reality we build in our mind about equity, may not be the whole truth as we tend to jump to a conclusion without giving it a second thought. All humans tend to gather facts and then see those facts in the light of preconceived conclusions.

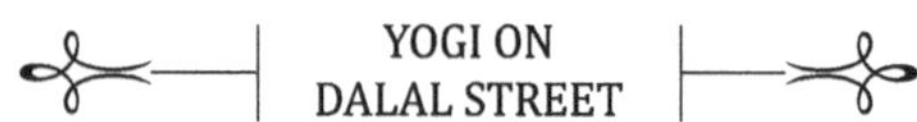

Consider, for example, an investor that hears about a stock tip from an unverified source, say an SMS or WhatsApp and is intrigued by the potential returns. That investor might choose to research the stock in order to "prove" its potential is real.

What ends up happening is that the investor finds all sorts of green flags about the investment such as growing cash flow or a low debt/equity ratio, while ignoring financially disastrous red flags, such as management integrity, corporate governance issues or dwindling market share.

People tend to have a preconceived notion or opinion about anything that they witness, leading to a judgment in their heads. As a result, people do not judge situations based on facts that they see but based on what their preconceived notions are. This first impression can be hard to shake because people also tend to selectively filter and pay more attention to information that supports their opinions, while ignoring or rationalising the rest.

A similar thing can be seen in investing where an investor seeks information that supports their original idea about an investment rather than looking for information that may contradict it. As a result, this Viparyaya (bias) can lead to faulty decision-making because the investor does not tend to judge the situation holistically, but only through a skewed perspective.

Have you noticed that you tend to give more weightage to the opinions of those who agree with you? Investors do this too. How often has one analysed a stock and later researched reports that supported their thesis instead of seeking out information that may prove them wrong. This has been termed as "confirmation bias" in behavioural finance.

How to avoid confirmation bias

Be a more evolved investor by performing the following checks:

- Take an independent decision based on firsthand information. Remove Asmita or ego. We should seek the truth over being right because if we disregard the truth long enough, we will eventually be proven wrong anyway.
- Check for basic Vidya or fundamentals of the company like valuation, market share, competitive environment, financial health ratios etc. Our opinion should be backed by knowledge of facts and figures rather than a preconceived notion.
- Have you invested in this stock or similar stocks before? If yes, then what was your investment outcome? If not, then screen similar stocks using a stock screener and back test the data for various time frames to arrive at a conclusion. Use Gyana to fight Viparyaya.

Overriding one's "need to confirm" or confirmation bias is a difficult task and takes time to develop. A Yoga investor, however, is aware of such pitfalls and enters the market armed with Gyana / Vidya keeping their Viparyaya or prejudices at bay.

Attaching oneself to an irrational peg

Most of us have a tendency to attach our thoughts and judgment to a reference point in the past (Raga and Dvesha), even though logically it may not be related to any event in the present. In the case of the equity market, one tends to attach a previous stock price as a reference point and judges a stock based on the deviation from that reference point. This can make investors base their decisions on irrelevant figures and statistics. Let us look at an example of this

Viparyaya and how it distorts the decision making process. This happens because at times we use an irrational peg or anchor to take decisions that have limited or zero relevance to the decision at hand.

Dhanteras and buying gold anchor

We are told that it is customary and auspicious to buy gold on days like Dhanteras or Akshaya Tritiya. Indians typically display great adherence to tradition. The illogical, even stubborn emphasis on buying gold on specific days is a classic example of such Viparyaya. While buying something new is associated with the celebration of festivals, the buying of gold on the aforementioned days is a completely irrelevant reference point created by the jewellery industry to maximise profits, which has nothing to do with tradition or devotion to God.

Many people find it difficult to buy gold during these specific days but due to cultural pressure, they incur debt by borrowing money or use credit cards in order to ensure the custom is duly observed. Although the amount spent on gold as jewellery or as investment should depend on what a person can afford or its potential upside, respectively, many people illogically anchor their decision to these specific days. People fail to see through the fact that gold prices get inflated due this artificial demand created by the fixation of the crowd to these so called 'auspicious' days, and fall prey to this price rise. Because buying jewellery is not something people usually do, they are more likely to purchase something that is around the 'custom' despite the affordability or reasoning. Such is the hold that Viparyaya has over our minds. This tendency to attach our thoughts and judgment to a reference point in the past, even though logically it may not be related to any event in the present, has been termed as "anchoring bias" in behavioural finance.

Anchoring in Investments

Many investors get pegged or anchored to a particular price of a stock, say their buying price, and are unwilling to exit the stock at any price below the buy price. While the volatility of the overall market can cause some stocks to drop substantially in value and allow investors to take advantage of short-term price movements, stocks are prone to decline in value due to changes in their underlying fundamentals. When stock prices decline rapidly due to deteriorating fundamentals, one must take cognizance of the developments and course correct by exiting the stock rather than waiting and allowing losses to intensify. Many times the prices end up being a value trap and share prices drop even further, creating a new low. Hence, one must not get carried away and invest trying to average out the stock at low prices, just because it is trading much below the buy price. Verify the credentials and reasons for its low price; compare it with the intrinsic value before taking the plunge. The basic aim of investment is to buy businesses at reasonable prices - near or below their intrinsic value.

Similarly, some investors anchor a particular stock at a specific price only and hesitate to buy at a price above the pegged price. The share price is a function of earnings, its growth as well as the quality and longevity of the growth. If the market is confident about the company's capacity to exhibit the estimated growth over a long period of time, the market will reward the share prices accordingly as long as the company delivers. The stock prices of Eicher motors and MRF, for instance, have been moving upwards for a long time.

How to avoid anchoring

In order to beat anch3oring Viparyaya or bias, one has to overhaul one's thought process. One should not anchor an investment decision to any specific price point but to fundamental characteristics. Seasoned investors conduct a thorough analysis of the investment idea based on a slew of parameters.

Beginners are advised to take the help of expert advice instead of taking a unilateral decision based on price points.

Gambler's Fallacy

Gambler's Fallacy refers to the mistaken belief or Viparyaya that the occurrence of an event is unlikely if it has happened quite a few times in the past. This thinking is incorrect, especially in the case of simple but independent events like the flipping of a coin or using of a slot machine.

A similar behaviour can be detected in investing thinking where investors feel that if a stock has gone up for a large number of trading sessions in the past, it is less likely to go up in the trading sessions in the future. Market participants feel that the stocks trading at or near 52 week highs are bound to come down. This tends to make them sell their position in the stock soon enough. They are of the opinion that the universal law of gravity - 'All that goes up has to come down' is true in this case. It must be noted that the laws of physics are not applicable to the equity market. Many market participants are under the impression that the stocks trading at 52 week lows are a steal at this price and will appreciate in future. One must not get carried away and invest in a stock, just because it is trading at a 52-week low, expecting it to move towards the 52-week high.

Many of us believe that the probability of the event decreases as every event passes by, but people don't realise that the past event does not always impact the future and that some events occur individually.

How to avoid Gambler's Fallacy

An investor must bear in mind that a change in stock price is independent of the movement on the preceding day. It is instead based on the solid reason/event which has caused the move. Investment decisions should be solely based on either fundamental analysis or technical analysis or a combination of the two. It must be remembered that one should not confuse Gambler's Fallacy with the concept of Technical Analysis, as the latter is based on multiple factors, rather than just the price trends, whereas the former takes into account only immediate past prices.

Selling winners and holding on to losers

Investors sell stocks too early when they have appreciated in price (without waiting for the stock prices to assimilate the real reasons for price discovery) while holding on too long to the stocks that have depreciated in price. A study indicates that investors are more likely to sell a winning position than a losing position. This Viparyaya or tendency harms the investment returns of the investors. Behavioural analysts also call this theory the 'Disposition Effect'. This theory, in short, refers to people's tendency to hang on to the losers too long but sell the winners too soon. This allows them to enjoy the feeling of winning faster and defer the pain of loss.

How to avoid Disposition Effect

Investors should not get carried away by short term price movements. They should instead concentrate on strong fundamentals. They should prepare a rule-based investment strategy without focusing on price movements. Active trades should have an exit strategy in the form of a trailing stop loss to protect their gains in the event of major crashes.

Adopting 'Vairagya' or the policy of 'doing nothing' after making an investment in profitable long-term businesses with a strong brand value and ignoring noise is also essential for an investor. This also ensures that one does not make investment decisions in haste.

Other Viparyaya in the equity markets

The share market is a place which makes princes out of paupers. Patient investing is the key to making this possible. This truth unfortunately makes room for the Viparyaya or various biases that distort reality. One of the biggest Viparyaya among investors is that the equity market is a shortcut to create wealth. They tend to forget the basic prerequisite viz., patience, in the process of becoming wealthy. Hence, in their pursuit of wealth, they end up losing their hard earned savings by frequent mindless trading. They then call the equity market a gambling den. In the equity market, investors invest in a business; they receive part ownership of the company, however small it may be, in lieu of the money they put in. They are entitled to hold claims on the assets of the company as well as a fraction of profits generated by the company in proportion to their stake. The price of the share fluctuates on a day-to-day basis, in response to the collective outlook of the market on the future earnings of the company. However small may be the value of the investment in the equity market at any given point in time, it still has some retention value and has the potential to grow big as the company prospers, unlike in a casino where if one wins the bet, one gains and loses one's money completely in case of a loss.

Another ill-found notion held by the public in general is that equity is just for wealthy people. The truth is that it is the only asset class, where a small investor can invest as small an amount as Rs 500 on a monthly basis in the form of an SIP. One does not need to have a corpus to make an investment as in the case of other asset

classes, especially real estate. In equities one can invest even in one share of a company.

People also feel that 'Today's small caps / mid-caps are tomorrow's multi-baggers.' It is partly true - but not all small/mid-caps have the potential to be multi-baggers. Multi-baggers, for those not familiar with the term, are stocks that multiply in market cap over a short period of time i.e. they become 10x or 100x over a few years. For a company to become a multibagger, it has to have a business that disrupts the established modalities or rules of doing business and still enjoys laurels from both the end consumer and the investor. The company has to have an innovative product and robust business model. If an investor can identify a company with such a product in its infancy, and hold its share for long, the investor is rewarded in terms of returns in multiples versus just in percentage terms. Even a well-researched, widely known large-cap company can be a multi-bagger if it has such an innovative product that challenges the market and sweeps the end consumers off their feet.

Conclusion

It is only human that we apply filters to the truth and make sense of reality. However, one must be mindful of biases and question whether these filters are distorting one's realities to a point that they become ill-founded notions or prejudices. Blindness to such prejudices can be harmful to one's wealth. One must be careful that they are not getting pegged to an idea, price, trend or notion. These notions may be difficult to surpass as they require regular practice of intense mindfulness. One must step back and question one's investing decisions to gauge if they are grounded in Vidya or coloured with Viparyaya. Yogic investing is simple but not easy!

Chapter 3

Vikalpa

VIKALPA

शब्दज्ञानानुपातीवस्तुशून्योविकल्पः

Shabdajnananupati vastushunyo Vikalpaha

It is a sort of hallucination followed in sequence by mere words or knowledge and which, in reality, is devoid of truth.

– 1.9 Patanjali Yoga Sutra

In the world of investing, people also suffer from Vikalpa or imagination. We can create an imagined world for ourselves based on our way of contemplation of facts. However, creating an imagined world without giving proper thought to the facts leads to biases. Vikalpa, like all other Vrittis, has 2 sides, viz., the Klishta Vikalpa and Aklishta Vikalpa. The harmful side or Klishta Vikalpa arises due to our wrong knowledge or Avidya to an extent that it is devoid of truth whereas the Aklishta Vikalpa helps to beneficially imagine new possibilities. It is important that we understand the difference between Viparyaya biases and Vikalpa. While Viparyaya is born out of misconception of facts through the filters that we apply, Vikalpa in its Klishta or harmful form is mere hallucination without any evidence of truth. To liberate ourselves from such Vikalpa or imagination bias, we must first understand it. Let us take a look at it in detail.

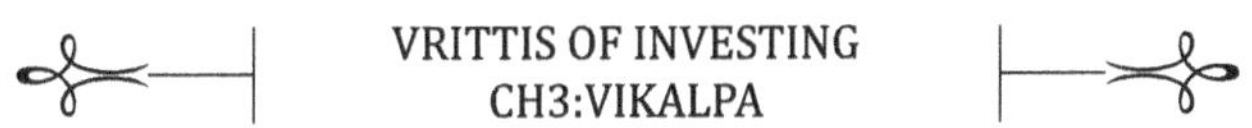

Value of money is different for different goals

Money is perceived on the basis of where we receive it from or where we plan to spend it. People do not understand that all money is the same and that it has no colour. Suppose one gets their bonus, or gets money as a gift on their wedding/birthday, wins a lottery, do you think they will treat it the same way they treat their salary? No, they will not. Even though money has the same buying power, irrespective of its source, investors typically attribute relative values to the money based on its source. As a result, investors may tend to be too conservative or too aggressive while investing. For example, investors might be investing all of their retirement savings in conservative avenues, such as fixed income instruments, even though most of the time, the returns on such investments might be less than the rate of inflation. On the other hand, they might invest very aggressively and indulge in speculation, if they have surplus funds that are derived from one-time gains.

People save money in a 'money jar' or 'savings account' for goals like buying a house or going on a vacation, which gives them a negligible rate of return while still carrying substantial credit card debt. Due to such Vikalpa or faulty imagination, investors like the psychological comfort they get from having money in their savings account giving them negligible or no return, even though they are transferring cash from the savings account to pay off the credit-card debt being charged in excess of 30% annually. Vikalpa separates the purchase made by the credit card from the payment and delays the payment. Thus, people consider it as an attractive option for payment.

Another way to look at it is that investors want to break up their investments into safe and risky investments in order to separate the effect of negative returns of risky investments on the overall

portfolio. However, in doing the above exercise, the investor does not realise that even though the portfolio will be separated, the returns and the net wealth of the investor would still be the same as if they held one large portfolio.

This imagination bias was developed by Richard Thaler, a nobel laureate in economics. He called it "mental accounting", which refers to a process wherein investors divide their pool of investment into separate baskets using mental accounts. This phenomenon is also known as the "two-pocket" theory.

How to avoid mental accounting

One of the ways to tackle the Vikalpa of mental accounting is by keeping track of all the expenses which include credit card bills, household expenses, travel expenses, etc., and observe the trend in one's spending over a period of time. One can compare it with the income one earns and ensure that all expenses are within the budget they set. One can translate one's mental accounting into something tangible and evaluate it for any loopholes. The aim is to ensure that nothing stays in our Vikalpa or imagination, and is instead recorded as Pramana.

Always have a plan for utilising surplus money in the best possible manner as well as account for all contingent expenses in the near future. Whatever unexpected money one gets should be utilised to pay debt, if any. In most cases, the interest on one's debt will erode any interest that one can earn in most savings accounts. While having savings is important, sometimes it makes more sense to forgo one's savings in order to pay off debt. Moreover, one can share money matters with an expert or a financial advisor, especially when one gets lumpsum, unexpected money.

An investor should understand that the end use of money should not be influenced by the source. Treat all income equally, irrespective of its source. Money is fungible and has no colour.

While Vikalpa is typically a negative imagination not backed by reality. We can use the same imagination to our benefit with the 'power of positive thinking'. Pratipaksha Bhavana, which reinforces the above thought, has been explained in the Abhinivesha chapter of the book. This Yoga concept helps to cut-off from the negative loop and harness positivity by looking at things differently.

Contrarian investor

Some investors incorporate a Pratipaksha Bhavana or contrarian element into otherwise conventional portfolios. Many of these apparently contrarian styles of investing are actually based on common sense and value investing principles. Contrarian investors may be defined as those who shun market trends and hyped investments and base decisions purely on their own analysis. A contrarian investor is looking for the undervalued and fallen stars that everyone else has abandoned. It is about thinking ahead of the crowd before the market realises the potential of a particular stock.

A contrarian investor enters the stock when others are feeling pessimistic about it and the value is lower than its intrinsic value. When there is a negative sentiment around the stock, there are possibilities of further price drops, and consequently, there is a high likelihood that the stock is battered beyond its fair value due to overreactions in the market. If the fundamental story is intact and if market noise has led to a steep fall in prices, the price will catch up sooner than later. Figuring out such distressed stocks and identifying the value in them is the area of expertise of contrarian investors. Simply put, buy when pessimism is at a peak and sell when optimism is at a peak.

However, the investor must do thorough due diligence, since such exercises may lead to value traps. The changed conditions may question the very basis of a stock's fair value. Each and every aspect should be checked to question the validity of the intrinsic value arrived at before taking the final decision to invest. Moreover, the investor should also increase the investment horizon and reduce the expectation in the short term due to the negative vibes surrounding the target investment. If convinced about the validity of their own investment rationale, such investors should also stagger their purchases to benefit from the low prices and negative sentiments about the target investment in the market.

Conclusion

Money is fungible and one must be mindful that one does not incur debt for a goal while keeping one's money idle for some other goal. The whole idea of wealth creation is to maximise overall portfolio gains and not do it in parts alone. Also, when the market is surrounded by negativity, it pays to practice Pratipaksha Bhavana, which teaches us to shift our imagination to positive ones; replacing desperation and pain with opportunities and joy. This is about steering the turbulent ship of emotions within us to arrive at the shores of self-healing. As the old saying goes, "Smooth seas do not make good sailors", an investor practising Pratipaksha Bhavana has to be a seasoned one. It is not advisable to practise Pratipaksha Bhavana when one is at the start of one's investing career. The investor has to be mature enough with reasonable experience in investing to distinguish between a value trap and a bargain. Without getting swayed away by the prevailing market price, one should be in a position to identify whether the available target is worth the price one is ready to pay or a trinket.

Chapter 4

Nidra

NIDRA

अभावप्रत्ययाअलम्बनातमोवृत्तिर्निद्र

Abhava pratyayalambana vrittir Nidra

The operation of the mind associated with the cognition of that which is non-existent is called sleep.

– 1.10 Patanjali Yoga Sutra

Sleep manifests when there is a predominance of Tamas and when Sattva and Rajas subside. It is a time of total inactivity and there is no knowledge of the external world. Sleep is a common activity for the mind and there are optimal times for sleep such as when the sun goes down. Some people sleep to 'escape the world' due to their worries and anxieties. However, too much sleep can make one dull and keep them from fulfilling their responsibilities. A person sleeping more than necessary is considered lazy or Tamasic in nature.

Sleep is an essential part of our day to day life, it helps us recuperate energies and refresh our mind. However, excess sleep or under sleep belong to the Klishta or harmful part of Nidra, which is undesirable. If we oversleep or undersleep, we feel drowsy for the rest of the day, our activities are restricted and we cannot give our

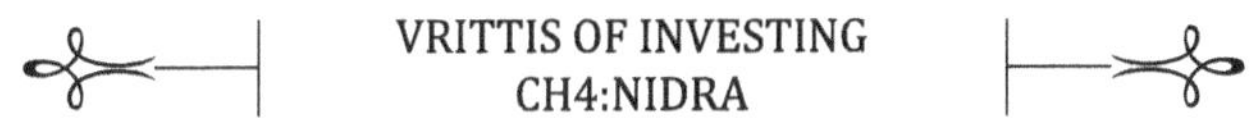

best performance. Right sleep which makes one feel fresh both on physical and mental level forms the Aklishta or beneficial side of Nidra.

People in whom the Nidra Vritti predominates, tend to not apply their mind and just go with the flow. To be in Nidra, is to be in a complete state of inertia without application of the mind. Let us look at a few investing behaviours that qualify as Nidra Vritti.

1/n diversification

It has been observed that investors use 'naïve' rules of thumb for portfolio construction. One such commonly encountered rule is the '1/n' approach, wherein they divide their investment amount equally into a range of available asset classes ('n' stands for number of options available). This sleepy approach ignores the specific risk-return characteristic of investments and the relationship between them. The investor substitutes the diversification principle based on the risk profile of an asset class by following a simpler approach of dividing assets uniformly among the investment option, without knowing the pros and cons.

Any portfolio skewed towards stagnant/underperforming asset classes, like FDs or gold, would produce low returns on a weighted average basis. With a higher share for these assets in the portfolio, the very purpose of beating inflation by a wide margin would be destroyed. Or otherwise, the equity portion of the portfolio will have to put in extra effort to bring the total returns above inflation which, given the volatile nature of markets, cannot always be guaranteed.

Another common form of 1/n diversification is the tendency to hold extreme portfolio allocations. On one side, an aggressive investor will hold an all-equity portfolio while on the other side, the highly conservative investor may not look beyond fixed deposits. This can be very well explained using the example of under sleep and over sleep. The aggressive portfolio would have very high exposure to equity or an even all-equity portfolio. The portfolio may overwork (i.e. undersleep) to produce high returns, but the associated risk may also be high, which could lead to untoward outcomes. Similarly, the risk averse portfolio is akin to oversleep, where returns would be hard to come by due to a paltry share of equity.

Have optimal balance of Nidra

Being a naïve investor, a person uninitiated in the mechanics of market operations has a limited know-how of the risk-return characteristics of asset classes. One's Nidra Vritti (both over and under sleep) prevents one from taking rational diversification decisions. Thus, it would be advisable for one to initiate investments using expert advice or simply invest one's money in various mutual fund schemes, based on one's risk profile.

Herd Behaviour

In Nidra, the involvement of the mind is minimal and the mind flows with the resting body to a subtle state of inactivity. Similarly, in investing we often see the tendency of individuals to mimic the actions (rational or irrational) of a larger group. Individually, however, most people would not necessarily make the same choice. This is also called 'herd behaviour' in behavioural finance terms.

There are a couple of reasons why herd behaviour happens. The first is the social pressure of conformity. One would probably know from experience that this can be a powerful force. This is because most people are very sociable and have a natural desire

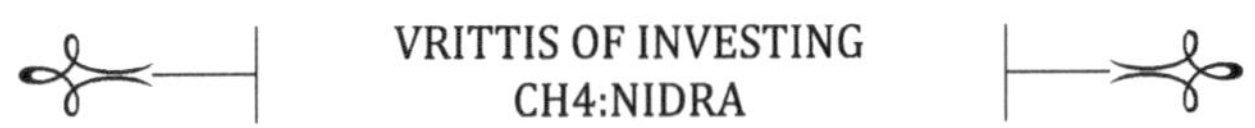

to be accepted by a group, rather than to be branded as an outcast. Therefore, following the group is an ideal way of becoming a member.

The second reason is the common rationale that it's unlikely that such a large group could go wrong. After all, even if one is convinced that a particular idea or course of action is irrational or incorrect, one might still follow the herd, believing they know something that one doesn't. This is especially true of situations in which an individual has very little experience.

Similarly, in the world of investing, people tend to excessively concentrate their investments in passive asset classes like fixed deposits, gold, etc., as most people they know do so. In equity markets too, we see people mimic actions of a larger group.

'Herd behaviour' was witnessed in the internet bubble in the late 1990s. Investors started investing huge amounts of money in internet-related companies just because other people were doing so. This was irrespective of the fact that a lot of these internet companies were running losses and had weak business models. This herd behaviour had led to huge amounts of investments in the equity market, leading to some highly overvalued companies. As a result, the asset bubble burst and the equity market crashed in 2000.

Protecting oneself from herd mentality

While it's tempting to follow investment trends, an investor is generally better off steering clear of the herd. Just because everyone is jumping on a certain investment 'bandwagon' doesn't necessarily mean the strategy is correct. Therefore, the soundest advice is to always do one's homework before following any trend.

One must remember that particular investments favoured by the herd can easily become overvalued because the investment's high values are usually based on optimism and not on the underlying fundamentals.

Inertia or procrastination

Investors often practice inertia, which means they fail to get around to taking action. It's the tendency of an investor to stray away from a predetermined course of action, despite having agreed to do so. In this pattern of behaviour, seen commonly in many aspects of daily life, the tendency to procrastinate dominates financial decisions.

Inertia can often act as a barrier to execution of an effective financial plan. Many investors think it is prudent to prepare a detailed financial plan to realise long-term goals, before stepping into the financial world. However, there is a huge gap between planning and implementation. This gap is Nidra or inertia. Without letting go of one's Nidra or state of inactivity, one cannot reap the true benefits of returns on their investments and thus may not be able to fulfill their desired goals.

Nidra can also lead to the tendency to procrastinate. If an investor has decided in principle to book profit or loss at 20% appreciation or depreciation, respectively, in price, it is not necessary that they may actually take this action. The Nidra in them prevents them from acting in alignment with what they had earlier decided.

How to avoid inertia

Letting go of one's inertia enables one to plug the gap between planning and execution. The share of Nidra should be ideally balanced, not too low, not very high. Nidra should be modulated at the right time to prevent one from going into a Tamasic state.

Perfect balance between activity and Nidra needs to be struck. In order to curb excessive Nidra one needs to be nudged repeatedly by an external factor. Since, Nidra is an inherent feature, one needs an outside force in the form of reminders like alerts, which constantly remind one of unexecuted tasks. The more frequently one is reminded, the higher the chances of being aware that action is necessary. This will eventually grow on one and help them negate inactivity or procrastination.

Conclusion:

Nidra or inactivity should have an optimal balance in life, neither too low nor too high. Nidra, in investment parlance, would mean displaying investment behaviour with minimal thought process or without exercising Viveka or discretion. Just like one must have the right amount of sleep as oversleep leads to low activity and undersleep leads to high activity and exhaustion, similarly, in investment terms, under allocation to equity leads to poor returns and high activity in equity can also be injurious to one's wealth, due to a high churn ratio. To overcome Klishta or the harmful aspect of Nidra one should avoid 1/n naive diversification, blindly following the crowd, inertia and procrastination. To leverage on the Aklishta or beneficial aspect of Nidra one should have the right allocation (based on risk profile) of fixed income and traditional asset classes like gold, which effectively reduces the overall portfolio risk.

Chapter 5

Smriti

SMRITI

अनुभूतविषयासंप्रमोषःस्मृतिः

Anubhuta vishaya sampramoshaha Smriti

Remembering past experiences is Smriti.

– 1.11 Patanjali Yoga Sutra

All conscious experiences leave an impression on the individual and are stored as memory, whether good (Aklishta) or bad (Klishta). It is not possible to tell if a memory is true, false, incomplete or imaginary. Just think about the retelling of any past event – different people recall different 'facts' and sometimes disagree on the details of what happened. Our inherent biases creep into memory and distort them, making them rather unreliable as sources of accurate knowledge. One may also ask why should memory be considered a Vritti that has to be transcended? Is memory not where all our experiences and knowledge is stored? Actually, when it comes to Yoga investing, the word 'memory' is Klishta or harmful when it distorts one's rational thinking. It is important to become aware of how memory creates biases that lead to unsound investment decisions. Let us understand the Klishta aspect of Smriti in greater detail:

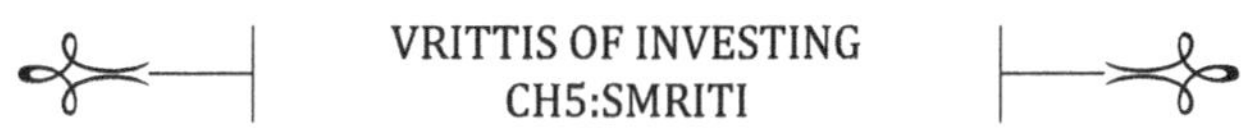

Prediction looks easy in hindsight

Many individuals feel as if something that has happened now could have easily been predicted in the past, even though it was not possible to have predicted it. In hindsight, a lot of things seem to be quite obvious. Once an event has occurred, we tend to explain the occurrence with the help of patterns that had been witnessed in the past using Smriti. This makes us feel that these patterns could have helped predict the situation earlier. What we don't realise is the fact that it would not have been so easy to predict actually.

Smriti gives one a sense that, after something happens, one somehow 'knew it all along'. This occurs because actual outcomes are more easily understood and recalled than many of the possibilities that did not actually turn out to be. It is this tendency that causes people to overestimate the accuracy of their predictions and brag. In the world of investing, Smriti may lead to a much more dangerous mindset, which is that of overconfidence, where investors believe that they are capable of easily predicting the direction of the stock. This leads to Asmita or ego and can have catastrophic consequences.

Asmita in the form of overconfidence is a commonly seen trait among successful but half-informed investors. Overconfident investors tend to overestimate their ability to identify winning investments. This overconfidence stems from their positive past experiences which look rosy and achievable in hindsight. Therefore, it is Smriti or memory that strengthens Raga or attachment to things that have given pleasure in the past and eventually leads to a bloated Asmita or ego. This Asmita allures one into a false sense of overconfidence in making a disproportionately large amount of money (maybe leveraged) in those investments which lead to a high risk in an attempt to make fast money. This has also been termed as "hindsight bias" in behavioural finance.

Characteristics of Smriti or hindsight bias are as follows

- Overestimating accuracy: Smriti of the past is clouded by the tendency to overestimate the accuracy of past decisions.
- A false sense of security: Overestimating the accuracy of past forecasts can lead to excessive risk-taking and can lead investors to plan for outcomes that may seem obvious, but actually involve much more uncertainty than they perceive.
- Recalling more good than bad: Many people subconsciously block Smriti or memories of poor investment decisions and recall successful decisions at a rate that far exceeds their actual results. In order to become a better investor, one should focus on objectively evaluating all of their investment decisions, both good and bad. Only by assessing one's weaknesses along with one's strengths can one avoid repeating past mistakes.

The ability to predict a bubble after the occurrence of an event is a classic example of Smriti or hindsight bias. A noteworthy example from recent history is that of the equity market crash in 2008. The equity market had reached a bubble stage due to an unrealistic valuation imparted to asset backed securities. As soon as the bubble burst due to these securities turning toxic, the market crashed. In hindsight, a number of investors claimed that the burst was predictable. However, only a handful of them would have actually sold their stock or booked their profit before the crash.

How to avoid hindsight bias

Investors should be careful while evaluating the unfolding of past events and connecting them to the current market conditions, especially when considering their own limitations to predict how

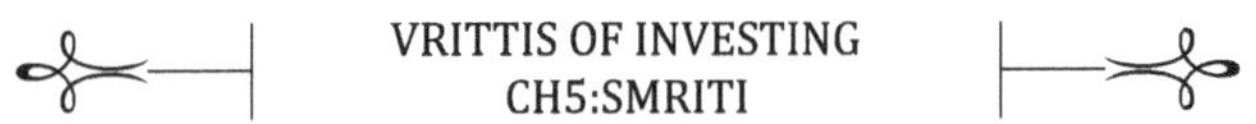

current events will impact the future performance of securities or the overall market. Believing that one is able to predict the future outcomes can lead to overconfidence, and this overconfidence can lead to choosing stocks not for their financial performance but for personal reasons. One should acknowledge this human limitation. This helps us stay focused on what we can control.

Recent Smriti or memories weigh heavy on the mind

Memories have a serious impact on investment behaviour especially of an equity investor. Memory represents impressions left by the conscious and unconscious experiences of an individual. These memories may be good or pleasant. The investor may have made money leading to Raga. The memories could also be unpleasant. The investor may have lost money leading to Dvesha. The outcome could even be mixed with some success and some failure. One would have made money but due to their impatient nature would not have been able to milk the opportunity, thoroughly.

Generally, the latest Smriti or memory would have a larger impact on the action than the one which one has tasted years back. This 'recency bias' often influences judgment. An investor would remember the loss incurred by them or a wrong trade enacted by them recently in a stock more vividly than the gains they had in the same stock, say a couple of months back. When they try their next trade in the same stock, it would be under the influence of their loss-making position. The Klishta Smriti or bad memories last longer than the Aklishta or pleasant ones.

This often prevents an investor from arriving at a logical conclusion by disrupting the ideal decision-making process. Say, for example, an investor purchases a stock for Rs 50 and over a period of one-and-a-half month, the stock appreciates to Rs 60.

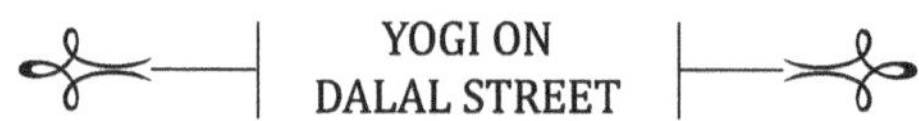

Having seen returns of almost 20% over this period, the investor books a profit. Over the next 15 days, the stock then climbs past Rs. 75. The investor would regret the action that caused a notional loss of Rs 15 more than the joy derived from a 20% gain in a matter of 45 days, despite understanding that the price spurt to Rs 75 would have been an exaggeration. In their next trade, they will think twice before squaring off their position entirely. The investor may defer selling the position on the expectation of booking more gains, which may or may not come, or they will spread their sell position over different price points to make the most of the rally. Several studies also suggest that the recency bias played a huge role in investor behaviour during the recent COVID-19 pandemic. People seemed to be highly influenced by the information projected in the media which led to how companies performed in the stock market. For example, as soon as lockdown was declared, the hospitality industry suffered a huge blow in the market as the investors were quick to sell shares. On the other hand, as soon as the news of a potential vaccine by a company began circulating, their stocks sky-rocketed.

How to avoid the effects of recency

One of the ways in which one can avoid the influence of the recency bias on the decision-making process, is to follow the rule book strictly in letter and spirit. Set the rules and practice them in a disciplined manner, irrespective of the price movements. There may be some exceptions but there are high chances that sticking to the rule book would prevent the investor from falling into traps.

Just as Aklishta Smriti or beneficial imagination can act as a curative force in life, projecting or remembering fond memories over sad memories can set the positive thought process rolling. The

Klishta Smriti or bad memories can be selectively and constructively used to put checks and balances wherever required. The whole process of managing the good and bad memories using the Yoga principles comes with sustained practice.

Conclusion:

Smriti is a mix of both positive and negative experiences in the past thus influencing our decision making in the present, which decides our future. One has to take cognizance of all old experiences. However, the final decision should be made on the basis of bare facts put forward independent of the colours added by our past experiences. Smriti should be used as a tool to avoid pitfalls but should not colour one's decision making to the extent that it adversely impacts future prospects.

In essence, just as the goal of Yoga is to 'still' or 'silence' the fluctuations in consciousness, similarly the aim of Yoga investing should be to free oneself from various biases so that one can invest right. Yoga, in short, has much to offer to the one who wishes to become a wise investor.

Module 5

Chitta of Investing

Preface

चञ्चलंहिमनः कृष्णप्रमाथिबलवद्दृढम् |

तस्याहंनिग्रहंमन्येवायोरिवसुदुष्करम्

Chanchalam hi manaha krishna pramaathi balavaddrudham

Tasyaaham nigraham manye vaayoriva sudushkaram

For, the mind is fickle, rebellious, strong and stubborn, O Krishna. To control it, I think, is more difficult than controlling the wind.

– Bhagavad Gita, Chapter 6.34

Arjuna voices his dilemma on the fickleness of the human mind and questions Lord Krishna that the art of controlling the mind is difficult. We know by now that the central theme of Yoga Sutra is to still the Vrittis (fluctuations) in the Chitta (mind) which is not easy. It is evident from the very fact that it comes from Arjuna, a mighty meditator, who is said to have pleased Lord Shiva through his meditation. Lord Krishna responds to Arjuna's question in the next shloka.

असंशयंमहाबाहोमनोदुर्निग्रहंचलम् |

अभ्यासेनतुकौन्तेयवैराग्येणचगृह्यते

Asamshayam mahaabaaho mano durnigraham chalam

abhyaasena tu kaunteya vairagyena cha grihyate

O mighty-armed son of Kunti, it is undoubtedly very difficult to curb the restless mind, but it is possible through suitable practice and by detachment.

– Bhagavad Gita, Chapter 6.35

Accepting what Arjuna has said, Krishna gives a conclusion. Though the mind is difficult to control, it is possible to control it by repeated practice under the guidance of a qualified guru by dissociation from the objects of immediate enjoyment that give short-term pleasure or Raga.

The equity market is a theatre for the free play of human emotions, a stage for the wild dance of the human ego (Asmita). Its workings reflect the fickleness that is the nature of the human mind, which is arguably the most complex structure in the universe. Yoga teaches us about the five states of Chitta or mind that range from a troubled or disturbed mind to a completely mastered mind. The good news, Yoga informs us, is that the mind can be coaxed to higher productive states that are conducive to the attainment of whatever it is that we seek to achieve in life.

It is the nature or Prakriti of the mind to constantly look for objects to play with. Prakriti does not allow a vacuum to be created in the mind. Once the mind rids itself of one thought or preoccupation, another immediately manifests. The mind can never become totally empty. It constantly looks for toys to play with.

It is easy to lose sight of the importance of mind-management in the process of wealth-creation because shifts in mental states cannot be gauged accurately and measured numerically. However, the mind and its effective use remain at the heart of all human undertakings, including wealth creation.

So, what are the various states of mind that Yoga aims to still or control? The Chitta or mind manifests itself in five different forms that have been named Kshipta, Mudha, Vikshipta, Ekagra and Niruddha.

The Kshipta Chitta is a wandering one. The mind is restless, troubled and jumps from one object to another under the influence of Rajas. It floats without rest among objects of love, fear and hatred like a feather in a storm. Such a mind shies from association with the wise as they are a constant reminder that life need not be all frenzied activity. The Kshipta state of mind is least desirable from the Yoga point of view or even dangerous as it is difficult to take important decisions in this state.

In the Mudha Chitta, the mind is dull and drowsy. It is that heavy and lethargic frame of mind when we want to do nothing and only get involved with things that do not require active attention. The Mudha state is one where the mind is in a state of sleep on account of Tamas. When one is mentally fatigued, one may say, "I need a break". All they want to do at that time is to be a couch-potato.

Vikshipta Chitta is an oscillating mind – occasionally steady but mostly distracted - unlike Kshipta. In this state of mind, one's attention is easily drawn here and there. The mind can concentrate for short periods of time, and is then distracted by a transient thought. Then again, the mind is brought back, only to be distracted once again. The Vikshipta state is one where one witnesses Sattva, the quality of poise and positivity, emerge temporarily only to be overpowered with Rajas or Tamas. One needs to develop concentration through gradual training of the mind to transcend this state.

In the Ekagra Chitta, the mind is one-pointed and concentrated. The Ekagra state is one of meditation. This is a state where Sattva or the mode of poise and positivity reigns, free from the influence of Rajas and Tamas. What this means is that one can focus on any task one undertakes and handle them perfectly. A person with an Ekagra mind works on matters at hand, undisturbed, unaffected, and uninvolved by distractions in any form. Such a person is fully present in the moment, committed to the cause and is able to attend to disturbances at their will. It's a desirable state of mind for one who sets out to achieve anything in life.

The last state of mind is the Niruddha Chitta or a state of arrested mind. The Niruddha state is one where all Vrittis of the mind are calmed. It is the ultimate state of mind from the Yoga perspective. While Yogis aim for the Niruddha state, it's very difficult to achieve. The Niruddha state of mind is only attained through constant and disciplined practice.

The behavioral aspect of investing or investor psychology plays a critical role in making sound investment choices. How we make an investment decision largely depends on the way we think and behave. One will have to train the mind, step by step, stage by stage, and lead it from the fickle state (Kshipta) or completely inactive stage (Mudha) to the occasionally steady (Vikshipta) stage and then to the one-pointed (Ekagra) stage. Kshipta and Mudha are undesirable states of mind as contemplation and concentration of mind is not possible in these states. One needs to regulate the mind to higher states, like Ekagra and finally, Niruddha, in order to focus on things with clarity. The path to Ekagra passes through Vikshipta which is an inevitable state. The transition from the disturbed Kshipta state to an occasionally steady Vikshipta state can be done by regulating hyperactive Rajas to lower levels with determination and self discipline. The transition from an inactive Mudha state to Vikshipta state can be done by shedding excessive Tamas. Once the Vikshipta stage is achieved, one can focus on things albeit temporarily and with practice, progress to Ekagra through concerted efforts. Once the Ekagra state is mastered, one can eventually elevate to reach the last frontier of Niruddha.

The awareness of our mental states is a necessary prelude to reining in the wild dance of the mind, which is the primary tool at the disposal of the investor who seeks to create a fortune. The equity market is no place for the unstable.

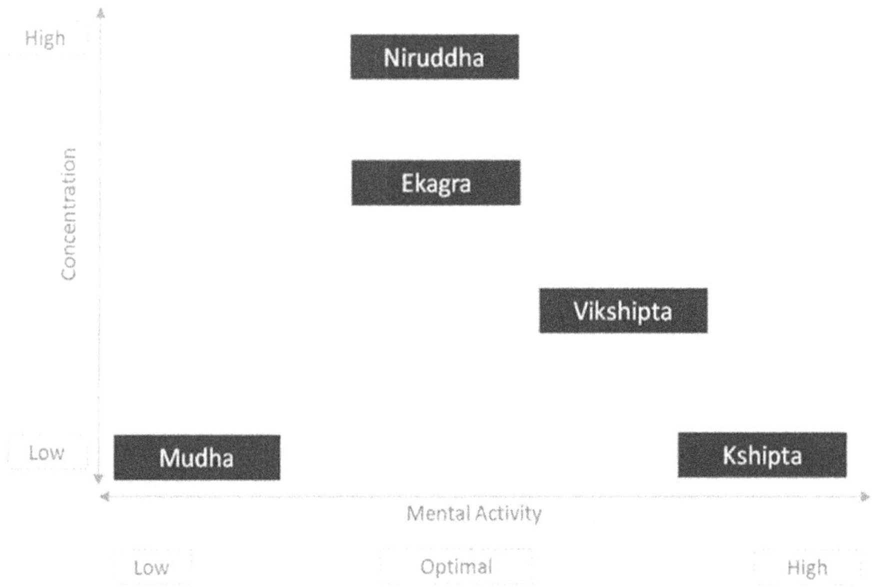

Chapter 1

Kshipta

KSHIPTA

नास्ति बुद्धिरयुक्तस्य न चायुक्तस्य भावना |

न चाभावयतः शान्तिरशान्तस्य कुतः सुखम् || 66 ||

nasti buddhir ayuktasya na cayuktasya bhavana

na cabhavayatah santir asantasya kutah sukham

One who is not in transcendental consciousness can have neither a controlled mind nor steady intelligence, without which there is no possibility of peace. And how can there be any happiness without peace?

– 2.66 Bhagavad Gita

We all know the story of Arjuna, when he is with the other Pandavas and the Kauravas, trying to aim at the eye of that little bird sitting on a tall tree. As the teacher asks each one, they talk about the tree, the leaves and many other things. It is only Arjuna who says 'I see only in the eye of the bird and nothing else.' And the teacher tells the others that this is where concentration helps. If one allows the mind to wander, one won't hit that target.

We are also easily distracted by that which captures our interest or which we find useful or intriguing for other reasons. But these

may not be our objective for the moment. So, in general, our concentration is very poor.

The modern mind is distracted in a thousand ways through alluring images thrown at it through various media. An investor in the Kshipta state succumbs too easily to rumours and 'sure tips' floating in the market. The stories of people coming to grief after short encounters with the equity market are more often than not, in this state of mind. Such a mind is under the spell of the hyperactive 'Rajas' Guna. All humans in the state of ordinary consciousness experience the Kshipta state. If one watches one's own mind carefully, one is sure to become aware of this tendency to jump from one thought to another in response to the stimuli provided by the world.

A Kshipta or wandering mind pays little attention to investments as it involves a serious thought. Instead, the mind is troubled with impulsive financial decisions taken at the spur of the moment. Big purchase decisions are taken and credit cards are used in a jiffy to satisfy temporary needs while neglecting bigger investment needs. Savings as a result, are minimal as they are typically a residue that remains after what has been spent. Such people also fall prey to mis-selling of financial products or end up investing based on hearsay. A Kshipta mind, due to its poor attention span, shies away from financial or effective tax planning as they require meticulous planning and discipline in execution. It typically ends up making tax related investments, if any, at the last minute, randomly picking up investment vehicles as suggested by one's fellow colleagues.

It is not surprising that people in the Kshipta state of mind get carried away by the potential returns that an investment can offer. They make little effort to find out about the fundamentals of the investment vehicles, the process involved and the factors

that multiply the investments to create tangible wealth. They have moments of insecurity as well as phases when they suffer from an unfounded sense of confidence with their meagre knowledge. They are prone to accept advice from unreliable sources, which often lands them in a soup. Equity may happen to be just one of the many investments they make. Such people invest in equity based on so called 'tips' and they actively indulge in all sorts of avoidable stocks hoping to make fast money. The Kshipta or noise traders are prone to investing in stocks without fundamentals and which are highly speculative and volatile in nature like penny stocks. Penny stocks are stocks that have an extremely low price, say upto Rs. 10. They also have a small market capitalization and are relatively illiquid as well as under researched. Kshipta investors get attracted towards penny stocks in order to get rich quickly. Due to their unstable mindset, they easily fall prey to the bogus investment rationale given by the unscrupulous elements in the equity market as well as the low prices. They also get carried away by the high volume of shares they are able to purchase for a relatively small amount. Say, Rs. 50,000 invested in a Re 1 stock yields them 50,000 shares, which becomes their anchor point. Kshipta investors believe they can easily double their investment to Rs. 1,00,000 with an increment of just Re 1 in the price of the stock. They also feel that they have a comparatively lower downside i.e. just Re. 1 and an unlimited upside. This is generally not the case since penny stocks are those that are mostly discarded by market participants due to poor performance, corporate governance issues or malicious financial statements and thus, seldom have a bright future.

Kshipta investors lack rational thinking and get carried away with early successes achieved, i.e. what has been called 'beginner's luck'. This convinces them that they have mastered the art of making money through equity investment. With their newly gained confidence, they double up their investment or trading corpus only to lose money in the long run.

A lot of new investors in the Kshipta frame of mind get agitated easily, which gets reflected in their investment behaviour as well. They become 'noise traders'. A landmark 1986 paper by the economist Fischer Black, stated that 'noise' ought to be distinguished from 'information' and that a disproportionate amount of trading occurs on the basis of noise rather than evidence. Most noise traders believe they are making sound investment decisions when they follow market noise. The trades made by noise traders are not based on any fundamental data; they usually try to jump on the bandwagon and react quickly when they think noise is taking the market in a particular direction, and subsequently, they make poor decisions by overreacting to good and bad news.

Noise traders, in particular, have a reputation for deciding on the basis of trending news, apparent surges or declines in prices or word of mouth rather than fundamental analysis, which is what experienced traders rely on.

The noise traders in Kshipta state of mind usually imitate other traders and follow the trends blindly. When they see a price rise or fall, they jump aboard as they trust other traders' moves more than the fundamentals. Therefore, they mimic other players even when they are erring. They place themselves in risky positions, like those other traders who are also full of hyperactive Rajas. Since Kshipta traders are always watching price movements of equities and listening to other aspects of noise in the market, their trades can often have a short-term effect on that particular stock/equity in the market, especially penny stocks. Constant buying and selling done by these traders causes an illogical increase in price and volume volatility.

A person with a Kshipta mind happens to fall into the "noise" trading trap because they fail to understand that analysis, forecasting and patience are the pillars that make investments enjoyable and remunerative. They are followers of the floating messages that urge them to trade in specific stocks in order to multiply money in short periods of time. Being highly Rajasic or energetic, such investors jump in on the word go without cross checking the credentials of the source.

In other words, the market will always have a crowd where the blind leads the blind. Sound knowledge of the fundamentals is, of course, the key to curing this blindness. In Yoga terms, this state of sub-optimal investing predominantly stems from Avidya or ignorance. It can be seen in traders irrespective of their education levels because of their lack of understanding or lack of knowledge of the equity markets in particular. Kshipta traders fail to understand the pulse of the market. They do not understand the investment potential of the target equity but end up buying the stock when it moves up, often when the stock is in the last leg of the run up.

Taming the Kshipta mind

The best way to control a Kshipta mind is to break down one's investing into actionable items and focus on doing just one thing at a time.

1. **Pay down the liabilities:** One should take a step back and before one thinks about investments or building assets – they must think about their liabilities and how they will deal with them. Stay away from credit card debts. This is especially for the Kshipta minds as they have a habit of making impulsive purchase decisions. They must use their credit card wisely and only if they have a confirmed

source for paying it back before the due date. They should never ever get into a credit card debt problem. Credit cards are almost always spent on stuff one could live without and the high interest rate makes one's outstanding loan amount burgeon into a huge sum of money, if no corrective action is taken. Credit cards in the hands of instinctive buyers, like those with Kshipta minds, is surely a recipe for disaster. They end up purchasing all those goods which would satisfy their momentary urges but would be a surplus after some time. One should take stock of all of one's loans and think of getting into the habit of putting aside some money every month and get the liability off their books. This discipline will help them build savings once they get out of debt.

2. **Manage temptations in spending:** If one buys things they don't need, they will soon sell things they need. One can make more money not only by investing or taking up a second job but also by resisting the temptation to go out and just splurge. As the saying goes – a penny saved is a penny earned. To be a successful investor, one needs to use due diligence. Spending wisely is not about being miserly, but about being smart. One should monitor one's spending habits and give second thoughts on whether this is something they need and if it is something they can afford. One can keep a note or download an app that keeps track of one's expenses as well as decide on a threshold that they will never breach.

3. **Avoid trading:** Those with a Kshipta or disturbed state of mind should stay away from trading in the equity market. They shouldn't speculate or trade based on hearsay and should avoid penny stocks. Unlike what most people believe,

the odds of winning are always against the trader. Invest wisely for the long term in structurally and fundamentally strong stocks.

4. **Seek help of an expert financial advisor:** One should take the help of an investment advisor to plan one's financial goals and set aside the required sums of money towards one's goals. Spending should be a result of what is left after savings and not vice-versa. One can practice forced savings towards one's goal by starting an equity or mutual fund SIP within a few days of their salary credit. This will automatically reduce the corpus left for spending and will force them to spend wisely. One can also set a calendar in their phone for quarterly reviews of their investments with the advisor. One should ask oneself and one's advisor if their investments are on track? Is their spending in check? Do they need to step up their investments?

Conclusion

Investors with a troubled state of mind should stay away from trading in the equity markets since they could easily get carried away with the volatility in the markets. A Kshipta mind's impulsive nature forces investors to buy or sell the investment without getting into the reasoning or understanding the fundamentals. They get very nervous when observing price movements. They do not even add when the prices are trending low due to the fear of further correction. Many times they end up selling when they should have either bought or added more.

They should therefore, focus on investing preferably with the help of a seasoned expert with proven credentials, i.e., a financial advisor. They should buy stocks like they invest in fixed deposits and forget about them for 5 years or invest through SIPs without looking at the price points. One should remember that investment in equities is like buying groceries - a fixed amount every month, and not like one buys a fancy phone, once in two years!

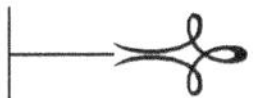

Chapter 2

Mudha

MUDHA

इन्द्रियाणि पराण्याहुरिन्द्रियेभ्यः परं मनः ।

मनसस्तु परा बुद्धिर्बुद्धेर्यः परतस्तु सः ॥ ४२ ॥

Indriyani parany ahur indriyebhyah param manah

manasas tu para buddhir yo buddheh paratas tu sah

The working senses are superior to dull matter; mind is higher than the senses; intelligence is still higher than the mind; and the soul is even higher than the intelligence

- 3.42 Bhagavad Gita

A dull or lethargic state of mind is known as Mudha. One in a Mudha state is not suited to concentrate. During this stage, the mind is not acquiring any new knowledge. It is the quality of dullness or lethargy in which the mind lacks alertness with little or no interest in any activity, physical or mental. No productive work can be expected to be completed by the one in the Mudha state of mind. One may notice that Mudha is related to Tamas, or one may find a relationship between Nidra and Mudha. To put things in perspective, Mudha is a state where the mind is Tamasic and just short of Nidra, where consciousness is non-existent.

In fact, all these concepts are interlinked and coming to know these linkages will help one to progress to a higher state of mind through self-awareness.

Similarly, in the Mudha state of investing, one lacks the inclination to take efforts towards investing in high-yielding asset classes. Savings are left idle in bank accounts or one invests in sub-optimal asset classes that are not in line with one's risk appetite or financial goals. As the attention levels are really low at this stage, the very thought of planning for future goals and investing optimally simply does not arise. One tends to simply park their money earned in a savings bank account or at best one invests in traditional asset classes, like gold or real-estate, like their parents did. As this state is highly Tamasic, one tends to be in a passive state mentally and physically. The ideal way to leverage this state of mind is to look at passive ways of investing right. To do so, one needs to acknowledge and be self-aware of one's financial health. One also needs to consciously upgrade one's Vidya about more contemporary investment avenues, both in debt as well as equity. As a person in this mental state is not in a position to undertake active investment decisions, one must look at options of passive yet better yielding investments which will not only protect one's capital but also provide them with real-returns. Let us dwell upon the details of such investment avenues, both in debt and equities.

Types of Debt mutual funds:

1. **Liquid Funds** invest in highly liquid money market instruments. These consist of investments ranging from 1) few days to a few weeks and 2) 1 month to less than 1 year. These funds provide a low yield and are ideal for very

short to short term parking of money. They are suitable for investors who are ready to take a marginally higher risk for slightly higher returns.

2. **Short-term funds** invest mainly in debt securities with an average maturity of one year to 4.5 years; suitable for conservative investors with low to moderate risk appetites and an investment horizon of a few years. Given the higher investment horizon, these funds offer higher returns as compared to the above mentioned liquid funds.

3. **Dynamic bond funds** invest across all classes of debt and money-market instruments across various maturities. The portfolio reflects the interest-rate view of the fund manager, thus ideal for investors who don't want to take a call on future interest-rate movements but still want to benefit from any positive movements.

4. **Credit-opportunities funds** invest predominantly in corporate bonds and debentures of varying maturities. These funds are sought by investors with a moderate risk appetite and medium- to long-term investment horizon.

5. **Income funds** invest in corporate bonds, government bonds and money-market instruments with an average maturity of 4.5 years or more. These funds are highly vulnerable to the changes in interest rates and suitable for investors who are ready to take high risk and have a long-term investment horizon.

6. **Short-term, medium term and long-term gilt funds** invest in government securities of short term or medium to long-term maturities. These funds do not have default risk since the bonds are issued by the government. The NAVs of these fund schemes fluctuate according to the changes in interest rates and other economic factors. These funds

have a high degree of interest-rate risk, depending on their maturity. The higher the maturity of the instrument, the higher the interest-rate risk.

7. **Fixed-maturity plans (FMPs)** are closed-end debt mutual funds which work almost like a fixed deposit. They invest in debt instruments with maturities of less than or equal to the maturity date of the scheme and thus are a good option for conservative investors.

Unlike traditional investment avenues, like Fixed Deposits, the above-mentioned investment vehicles in debt ensure a relatively better yield with higher liquidity. All one has to do is be aware of these instruments and invest based on one's time horizon to invest. Now, let us explore some passive yet high yielding options to participate in equity as an asset-class.

Types of Equity mutual funds:

1. **Large Cap funds** carry relatively low risk as a minimum of 80% of the fund is deployed in large caps. Large cap companies are the top 100 companies by market capitalization which are by and large well-researched, well-managed and with a stable growth outlook.

2. **Mid Cap Funds** have a mandate to invest at least 65% of their assets in midcap companies. Mid cap companies are companies whose market capitalisation ranks between 101 to 250. These are mid-sized companies with relatively better growth potential.

3. **Small Cap funds** are required to invest a minimum of 65% of their funds in small caps. Small caps are companies whose market capitalisation ranks between 251 and beyond.

These are relatively smaller companies with a high risk-high return potential.

4. **Large & Mid cap funds** have a mandate to invest a minimum of 35% of their fund in large and mid-caps each.

5. **Multi Cap funds** contain a mix of large caps, midcaps and small caps with mandate to invest minimum 65% in equity. Such funds provide the flexibility to the fund manager to invest based on the prevailing market conditions.

6. **Dividend Yield funds** invest in dividend yielding stocks or stocks that pay periodic dividends.

7. **Value Funds** follow the value style of investment. These schemes are mandated to maintain a 65% allocation to equities that the fund manager believes are undervalued.

8. **Contra Funds schemes** follow the contrarian investment strategy taking contrarian view and have a minimum 65% allocation to equities.

9. **Focused Funds** invest in a maximum of 30 stocks. The scheme would mention which market cap it tends to focus on (multi-cap, large-cap, mid-cap, small-cap).

10. **Sectoral/ Thematic Funds**, as the name suggests, invest a minimum 80% of their assets in an equity of a particular theme or a sector e.g. infrastructure or PSUs or banking sector etc. Sectoral or thematic funds are generally considered risky for retail investors because their fortunes depend on the performance of a particular sector.

11. **ELSS (Equity Linked Saving Schemes):** ELSS are tax-saving mutual fund schemes with a lock-in period of three years and a minimum investment of 80% of the total assets in equities.

The above mentioned equity oriented mutual funds have the potential to offer higher returns as they are actively managed by a professional fund manager. One may also choose to participate passively in equity or Gold via Exchange Traded Funds (ETFs). However, unlike equity funds that are actively managed, these ETFs mimic the performance of the underlying like index or gold. The best part about investing passively via equity mutual funds or the ETF route is that it requires only a one time effort to identify a good performing fund or ETF and choose to invest in lump-sum or systematically via SIP route. One can relax and still watch one's money grow in the long-term without getting actively involved.

Taming the Mudha State

To appreciate equity one needs to have the basic knowledge or Vidya about equities. The Mudha state can be utilised as an opportunity to gain Vidya and step into equities slowly and gradually. One way of doing this is by practicing paper-money investing virtually without the use of hard currency. One can create an artificial virtual portfolio and monitor its performance without the risk of losing money. This will allow time for the investor to reflect on stock selection made and judge the soundness of the rationale adopted.

This offers good training and practice before actually entering into the real world of investing. If one is unsure about the performance of equity, one can fearlessly create a virtual portfolio and study the fundamentals of that specific equity before investing in real stocks. For a new investor or an investor who is surrounded by negative emotions, this is a good place to start the journey. This would enable an investor to get the feel of how equity markets operate and hone their skills, just to build the much needed confidence before they go in for the real experience. Similarly, one can use virtual portfolios to test one's strategies before applying them in real markets. Once an investor feels confident of one's investing skills, they should come out of their Mudha state and get ready to enter the stage of Vikshipta.

Conclusion

The path of Yoga is a path of conscious disciplining of the body, mind, intellect and emotions. It is not a path of a mystic but that of a 'doer or karta' who can consciously elevate themselves through clear and conscious efforts. Self-awareness is the first step to steer oneself from Mudha to the Vikshipta state. In order to do so, one must shed the lethargy of staying in a state of financial negligence and gain Vidya of contemporary yet passive forms of investing like debt or equity mutual funds that invest one's money with the expertise of a fund manager. One may also choose to invest passively via ETFs in gold or an index of one's choice.

Chapter 3

Vikshipta

VIKSHIPTA

बन्धुरात्माऽऽत्मनस्तस्य येनात्मैवात्मना जितः।

अनात्मनस्तु शत्रुत्वे वर्तेतात्मैव शत्रुवत् ॥ 6.6 ॥

bandhur ātmātmanas tasya yenātmaivātmanā jitaḥ

anātmanas tu śatrutve vartetātmaiva śatru-vat

For those who have conquered the mind, it is their friend. For those who have failed to do so, the mind works like an enemy.

– 6.6 Bhagavad Gita

When one's mind is focused and yet relaxed, that's when any art is perfected. The Vikshipta mind is mostly distracted but intermittently focused. This is the state of mind when one is wide awake and alert, neither noticeably disturbed nor dull and lethargic. Most people are in this state and people who have taken the plunge into equities are no different. Such investors come to believe that equity as an asset class can help them build wealth but are distracted by market noise and often act prematurely on the spur of the moment.

This is a superior level, as compared to Kshipta and Tamas' state of mind, which is in the process of being trained to concentrate. The hyperactive 'Rajas' Guna has been reduced to active 'Rajas' and the

236

gross 'Tamas' Guna has been improved to conscious control and focus on its activities. The transformation has happened with the help of mind control; the mind is in a state of receiving information and processing it occasionally. In Vikshipta state, the mind is applied to a certain activity and pulled back in case it drifts away.

In Vikshipta state, the investor has gathered sufficiently good knowledge of different asset classes, portfolio management and asset allocation. The knowledge along with controlled activity makes one create a portfolio of various assets/ sectors with proper asset allocation. Being Rajasic or excitable in nature, the investor in Vikshipta state is curious, reading about various opportunities and alternatives, understanding various asset classes/ sectors, and their developments to identify the best investment target. One also keeps one's eyes and ears open to grasp the developments around - both political and economical. The investor applies their knowledge to assess the impact of all developments on the portfolio.

As stated previously, 'noise' ought to be distinguished from 'information'. Unlike a Kshipta investor, a Vikshipta investor is in a better position to differentiate between information and noise. As the Vikshipta mind is occasionally steady but mostly distracted, it is not totally in a state to take full cognizance of the news and respond to the situation.

A Vikshipta mind can, however, be trained to become a better investor or trader and eventually progress towards an Ekagra mind or one-pointedness. Such an investor has the right intent in mind and follows markets regularly. Now, all one has to do is control one's urges to react and stay invested in the long-term by assessing the impact of the news on the fundamentals. One has learned to differentiate wheat from the chaff or in market parlance, 'noise' from 'information'. The investor has the capacity to analyse whether the event makes any structural change in the investment theme and acts accordingly. The Yoga Mantra for dealing with noise-created distraction is to rely on stocks with a strong fundamental and structural story. The investor must not get too disturbed with short term ups or downs and enjoy the noise instead of getting distracted by it. This in Yoga terms, is called Nishpanda Bhav.

Nishpanda Bhav

The cultivation of Nishpanda Bhavna involves listening to sounds without analysing, judging or evaluating the sound waves. This is passive listening. Passive listening consciously stops the analytical functioning of the intellect and disconnects emotional response for that duration. This facilitates the mental space for relaxation. The Yogic investor takes the practice of Nishpandha Bhav to the equity markets and passively listens to all that is happening around, without getting troubled. Importantly, he stoically refuses to take any action in the equity market on the basis of noise around him.

One must know that tracking the day-to-day movements of the equity market is nothing more than a distraction from investing.

Do keep in mind the following:

Don't ditch the process and plan. If one's plans were soundly constructed, they would factor in market movements. The decision to stick with the plan one decided upon is an important component of potential future investing success. No one wants to live through a negative investment performance but it is a part and parcel of the game.

Discuss the plan and related concerns with a financial planner. A good planner knows one's personal situation and approach to risk. If one has a financial plan, the financial planner will explain the

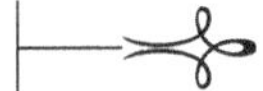

impact of the current market situation to one's personal needs and goals. Viewing the big investment story in the context of one's own financial situation can help gain the perspective one needs to stay the course.

Conclusion

Overall, an investor in the Vikshipta state is in the learning stage. One has assimilated the principles of investing; understands them thoroughly and is in the process of applying them. In the process, one takes home a few good and a few bitter experiences. Much like Yoga, investing is better understood by those who practice it. In the process of learning, one is often tempted to bypass fundamental principles for which one has to pay the price. Such an investor learns the rules of the game by making mistakes and getting one's fingers burnt. Having learned the principles of investment, one wants to experiment only to find one was wrong and the core investment principles prevail in the long run. Every time one deviates from the laid down principles of investment, one pays the price either through losses incurred or lower profits. Such experiments help investors grasp the principles of investing and help them ingrain the intricacies of the game in their thought processes. Such is the step by step progress towards the next stage that has been called the state of Ekagra, the state of a seasoned investor. The Kshipta and Mudha mind has to mature through the conscious cultivation of concentration in order to reduce the volatility, indecisiveness, and unpredictability and graduate into a semi controlled state of Vikshipta, which is the halfway stop to the state of Ekagra.

Chapter 4

Ekagra

EKAGRA

देशबन्धश्चित्तस्यधारणा ॥ १ ॥

deshabandhashChittasya dhaaraNaa

Dharana is the binding of the mind to one place, object or idea.

– Patanjali Yoga Sutra 3.1

तत्रप्रत्ययैकतानताध्यानम् ॥ २ ॥

tatra pratyayaikataanataa dhyaanam

Dhyana is the continuous flow of cognition toward that object.

– Patanjali Yoga Sutra 3.2

Patanjali Yoga Sutra 3.1 & 3.2 mentions the importance of pointed concentration through Dharana and Dhyana.

The Ekagra mind is firm, focused and resolute. In this state, the mind is relaxed and bereft of most worries. The Ekagra state is achieved by concerted efforts taken by an investor to diminish the volatility and oscillation of the mind. The investor is equipped to focus and pay attention to every small detail of the object of study from all 360 degrees of perception. The chances of getting a distraction in this state of mind are almost negligible.

Investors in Ekagra state of mind care little for anything outside their sphere of interest; they are focused on reading, understanding and deliberating on their area of excellence. The 360 degree overview enables the investor to take a look at all the possible scenarios before deciding to invest.

Ekagra investors would have first considered all the asset classes, compared them and after considering all the pros and cons, decided to focus on one or two asset classes. They would prefer investing in equities due to the transparency and ease of transaction. They would have studied the fundamentals of a company, before they decided to proceed further and invest. They would wait for the investment rationale to play out before selling their shares. In this state of mind, investors are passionate about their investments; they have the performance of their investments on their fingertips, and know the investments like the back of their hand.

A sailor cannot control the ocean, but he can control himself and his ship. He studies water currents and weather patterns. He is aware of safe sailing techniques and has gained substantial experience. He knows when to sail and when to stay in the harbour. A successful sailor uses his intelligence. Similarly, a professional investor uses his head and stays calm. Amateurs may become excited or depressed because of their bets. Emotional reactions are a luxury that one cannot afford in the equity markets. Acting out of five Kleshas of Avidya, Asmita, Raga, Dvesha and Abhinivesha diminishes one's chances of success. One has to analyse their behaviour instead of acting out on their feelings. This is 'sound mind' investing.

The equity market moves up and down, regardless of what one wants. Success and failure depends on one's thoughts and feelings. It depends on one's mindset towards profit and loss, fear and greed as well as envy and boredom. Finally, everything boils down to how one handles the trade-off between risk and return. The only thing one can control is one's behaviour. This is all part of having sound investing psychology.

Contrary to the ways of an investor in the Vikshipta state, who dabbles in different investment avenues, the investor in Ekagra state first develops a financial plan, which starts with knowing one's goals and analysing one's current financial situation. The next step is risk profiling and finding out the suitable asset allocation within equities, required for goal completion. Based on these two parameters, one can take concentrated bets on stocks whose potential one is convinced about.

Goal-based investing

The first step in investing is to ensure one has a set of detailed and well thought out goals. This requires a proper estimation of each of one's goals and the path to achieve them. To attain Ekagra in one's investing journey, it is important that one understands the behavioural and financial reasons on why goal-based investing is important:

1. Decide future goals

As one looks into the future and decides on goals, often well in advance, it enables one to estimate correctly how much money one will need at different points in future. A proper plan would help one match one's expectations in life with one's ability to save. It will help one chart out the savings plan to build up the desired corpus for every specific need. This ensures that one avoids under-saving.

2. Take fewer liabilities for more disposable income

When one plans in advance, one not only plans the goals but also tentatively accounts for any liabilities which might arise in future.

This helps one avoid a liability altogether or prune it to the extent possible by starting to save for it. The earlier one starts saving, the more time one gives the market to grow one's savings.

For example, imagine one wants cash to buy a new car — let's say Rs. 10 lakhs. The smarter way to do it is by not taking a loan on it where one pays interest but saves up ahead of time. If one even saves Rs. 20,000 monthly for two years, one would end up saving Rs. 5.4 lakh assuming a 12% rate of return. This ensures one takes less debt for the new car.

3. Data driven decisions leads to more precision

When one sets up an investment goal, for example a home of Rs. 1 crore after 10 years, financial planning would help one arrive at a suggested allocation based on one's time horizon i.e. 10 years and how much they need to save on a monthly basis to reach that goal (Rs. 1 crore). It also takes into account the initial corpus one may have already saved for the goal. When one takes guesswork out of one's plan, the probability of reaching one's target is very high.

4. Leverage mental accounting bias

Goal-based investing leverages mental accounting bias to improve one's investing behavior as explained in the Aklishta or beneficial side of Vikalpa Vritti. Mental accounting means that one treats money differently based on the source or purpose, rather than view it in the aggregate. While this could lead to unwise decisions as it may limit a holistic view of one's finances, one can also use mental accounting to their advantage. By creating many different mental accounts in the form of goals, one ensures that one is saving optimally for each of them — and does not rely on one account to cover all one's required future liabilities.

Conclusion

For an investor, the Ekagra state of mind is the best state for working on investment goals. In this state of mind, an investor looks at the investment goals objectively. Having considered every aspect of the investment with minimal distraction, they have thorough knowledge about the same. After the investment is committed to, the investor seldom gets affected by the noise around. They look through the developments around with objectivity, with Vairagya bhava.

Also, the key characteristic of this state of mind is that not only can the investor be goal-focused, if they are convinced about an investment story, they would have the courage to take a huge position in those companies thus taking a concentrated bet on them. Having understood the potential of the pharmaceutical sector way back in 2008–2009, smart investors created serious wealth by taking concentrated bets and staying put till the story unfolded.

Thus, like an Ekagra investor, in the goal achievement path, one shouldn't be disturbed till the goal is reached as focusing on the goal alone is the key characteristics of this state of mind. One must follow Swami Vivekananda's advice: 'Uttishthata jagrata prapya varan nibhodata' which means 'Arise, awake and stop not till the goal is reached.'

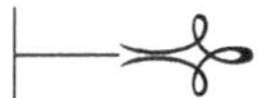

Chapter 5

Niruddha

NIRUDDHA

तदासर्वाअवरणमलापेतस्यज्ञानस्याअनन्त्यात्ज्ञेयमल्पम् ॥ ३१ ॥

tadā sarva-āvaraṇa-malāpetasya jñānasya-ānantyāt jñeyamalpam

This (the state of Niruddha) is a state of freedom where one knows all there is to be known.

– 4.31 Patanjali Yoga Sutra

The Niruddha state of mind is the ultimate state when the mind is in complete control of the individual. In fact this is also called a state of arrested mind. The state of Niruddha is a culmination of all positive states like

1. Minimizing the Panchkleshas of Avidya, Asmita, Raga, Dvesha and Abhinivesha
2. Walking the path of Dharma, garnering requisite Gyana, practising Vairagya to finally attain Aishwarya
3. Striking a balance between Rajas and Tamas Gunas to arrive at a state of Sattva

Developing beneficial or Aklishta Vrittis by conquering the harmful or Klishta ones and finally reining in the Vrittis altogether

Elevating oneself to the state of Ekagra and being in that state for a prolonged period of time

Thus, this is a state which is difficult to achieve but not impossible if one follows the steps outlined in Yoga Sutra. In the Niruddha state of investing, one has mastered the art of investing. Hence, not only does one know one's goals and the way to achieve it but has also mastered the art of stock picking. It's easier said than done. To master this art, one has to know how to choose good stocks with a reasonable margin of safety. In simple words, one chooses stocks that the market has undervalued and that have high growth potential. In this state, stock selection is based on fundamentals like promoter's background, commitment and vision, strengths of business and financials. Investors who use this strategy possess the Sattva Guna; they are thorough with the fundamentals of the investment and believe that the market overreacts to good and/ or bad news, resulting in market price movements, which would have nothing to do with the company's long-term fundamentals. Investors, who have achieved this state, are least concerned about day-to-day market movements. They revel in the feeling of Aishwarya and Vairagya Bhav, completely focused on the fundamentals, disconnected from the market noise around.

Investment is an art, it takes a lot of intuition and often some good fortune, but it ultimately falls back to Vidya or knowledge and skills that experience can impart. These few lessons are the jewels of experience of some of the greatest investors of all time. Perhaps to you, these renowned investors can be the instructors that help you strive towards Niruddha.

Warren Buffett

Warren Edward Buffett, the legendary value investor, turned an ailing textile mill into a financial engine that powered what would become the world's most successful holding company. He turned $6000 in the equity market into $85 billion. Making money was an early interest for Buffett; he sold soft drinks, worked in his family's grocery store in Omaha watching which consumer goods were in demand. He would spend days together listening to what investors did and what they said in his father's broking outfit. At times he also did small jobs like delivering newspapers and washing cars and used his savings to purchase a few pinball machines. Warren Buffett became a player at the investment game at the young age of 11. By the time Buffett was 15, he already had a net worth of about the then $6,000.

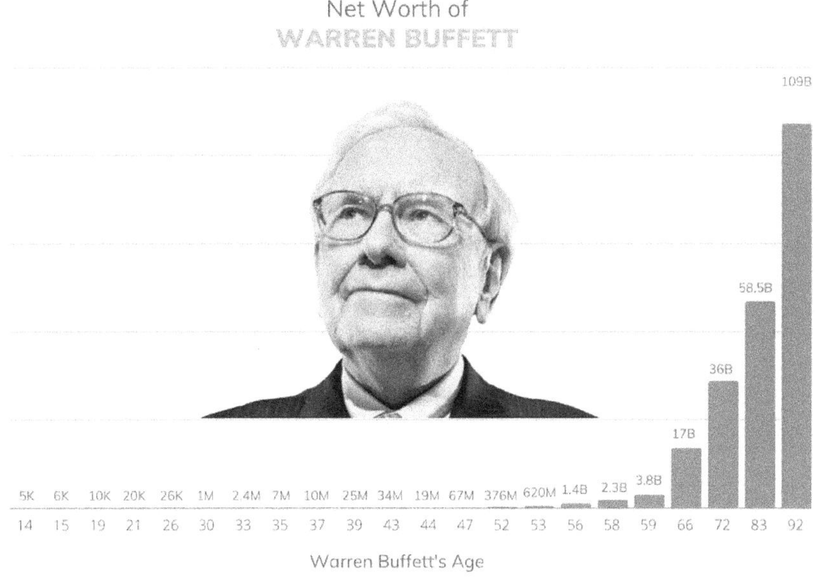

Source: finmasters.com

As of March, 2023 data from the Forbes website, Warren Buffets' Net Worth has grown to $106 billion. He ranked number four on the Forbes 400 list. Buffett added about $12 billion to his fortune in 2016, making him the biggest gainer among wealthy individuals in the U.S., according to both the Bloomberg Billionaires Index and a separate report from Forbes.

Warren Buffett's investment philosophy has changed over time and can generally be presented in two parts:

- Early Buffett (pre-1970): Buy at a significant discount to intrinsic value. 'Fair business at a wonderful price.'
- Late Buffett (post-1970): Buy companies at a price at or near intrinsic value, which can consistently increase their intrinsic value. 'Wonderful business at a fair price.'

He has said that the latter philosophy is far superior to the former and that it took him far too long to realise it. Buffett's investment philosophy has evolved over the course of his investing lifetime, and achieved Niruddha status.

Warren Buffet has a set of ground rules which he follows religiously. He does not try his hands in the markets, he does not speculate; he doesn't base his buy and sell decisions on the direction the stock market is going to take but rather upon what he thinks the company is going to do. To put it in simple terms, it is the bottom up approach. He purchases a certain big stake in the company after conducting thorough due diligence, using his own methods, based on his analytical skills. He ensures that the investments have a sufficient margin of safety and the target investment has the required moat to sustain the business for decades, if not ages. He eyes businesses where the management has a little role to play other than running the day-to-day show.

And lastly, he has sufficient patience to wait for the price at which he would like to invest; he waits for the deal to come to him at the price he wants, and on his terms. He does not over-stretch just because he has a cash surplus; he invests where he wants and when he wants, irrespective of the market movements. He strongly believes in 'Be greedy, when the world is fearful and be fearful when the world is greedy'.

Benjamin Graham

Benjamin Graham, who is also known as the father of two styles of investing- security analysis and value investing, was a British-born American economist and professional investor. Graham had many disciples in his lifetime, a number of whom went on to become successful investors themselves. Graham's most well-known disciples include Warren Buffett, William J. Ruane, Irving Kahn and Walter J. Schloss, among others. As per Columbia Business School records (where Graham was a student as well as financial educator), his investment fund averaged 17% compounded returns between 1934 and 1956. That amounts to around 31x the principal since inception.

Graham believed that the owner of equity stocks should believe that he is part owner of the company. He also recommended that an investor should spend time and effort to analyse the financial status of a company. He believed in fundamental analysis and sought out companies with strong balance sheets, low debt or above average profit margins and huge cash flows. If a company was available on the market at a price which is at a discount to its intrinsic value, a 'margin of safety' exists. This makes it suitable for investment.

Sir John Templeton

John Templeton consistently earned impressive returns over 60 years of his life in the equity markets. He had pioneered the use of diversified mutual funds. In the depressed market of 1939, Templeton borrowed $10,000 and bought 100 shares of every stock under $1 on the New York Stock Exchange. Not all stocks in this portfolio were profitable, however, 4 years later he sold 4 profitable stocks for $40,000. An investment of $10,000 in the Templeton Growth Fund in 1954 would've resulted in $2 million by 1992.

Sir John Templeton took value investing to an extreme, picking companies and industries that he believed were at rock bottom or at 'points of maximum pessimism'. He used a fundamental-driven, 'bargain-hunting' approach towards investing. He searched for shares that were selling below asset value due to temporary reasons, bought them and held them for years before selling.

Peter Lynch

Peter Lynch was an American businessman and stock broker. He managed the Fidelity Magellan Fund from 1977 to 1990, during which time the fund's assets grew from $20 million to $14 billion. Moreover, Peter Lynch beat the S&P 500 Index benchmark in 11 years out of those 13 years, achieving an annual return of 29.2%.

Lynch's most famous investment principle was, 'Invest in what you know', emphasising on the economic concept of 'local knowledge'. He felt that individual investors are more capable of making money from stocks than a fund manager, since they are able to spot good investments in their day-to-day lives before Wall Street.

Let us look at some examples of great investors in the Indian context.

Rakesh Jhunjhunwala

Rakesh Jhunjhunwala, a name synonymous with the Indian stock market, had a passion for investing that bloomed in his childhood. Even as a young boy, he would engage in animated discussions about the equity markets with his father. After qualifying as a chartered accountant, Jhunjhunwala plunged into investments in 1985, when the Sensex was a fledgling entity hovering around 150. He started with a modest sum of Rs. 5,000, a mere seed for the financial empire he would eventually build.

Popularly known as "RJ," Jhunjhunwala developed a unique investing style focused on identifying high-growth companies backed by strong promoters. He preferred concentrated bets, taking substantial stakes in the companies he believed in and holding them for the long term. A firm believer in value investing, he had the patience to wait for the perfect price and generally avoided the frenzy of initial public offerings. Before making any investments, RJ would meticulously analyze the company, its market share, pricing power, competitive advantages, and the vision of its management. This due diligence formed the bedrock of his investments, and once committed, he remained steadfast even amidst market volatility. Quarterly conferences served as platforms for him to engage with the management, ensuring his investments were on track as he envisioned. He readily acknowledged his human fallibility and learned from his mistakes, constantly evolving as an investor.

Over time, Jhunjhunwala's focus shifted from simply chasing profits to seeking quality investments. He recognized the influence of "non-company factors" on stock prices and adopted a holistic approach, meticulously analyzing not only companies but also the potential of the entire nation. He saw India's burgeoning skills, favourable demographics, accepting and patient culture, and abundant natural resources as fertile ground for future growth. He firmly believed in the burgeoning consumption potential of the Indian economy and the immense investment opportunities it presented. As he envisioned India transforming into one of the world's top three economies within the next two decades, he constantly championed the power of compounding returns offered by long-term equity investments. His chartered accountant background gave him the keen financial acumen needed to decipher and capitalize on these opportunities. Starting with a tiny seed, he cultivated a wealth that left many in awe, solidifying his reputation as a "Niruddha" investor - one who identified opportunities ahead of the curve and held onto them with unwavering conviction.

Rakesh Jhunjhunwala's legacy lives on in the fortune he amassed and the valuable lessons he imparted to aspiring investors. His story is a testament to the power of meticulous research, long-term vision, and unwavering commitment to the dynamic world of the stock market.

Radhakishan Damani

RK Damani is a famous Indian investor who has also been a mentor to Rakesh Jhunjhunwala. In addition to being a known equity investor, RK Damani is also the owner of DMart- a large, growing retail chain in India. He started his career as a speculator in equity markets at the age of 32, but later realised that trading/ speculating was not the best way to create wealth and one should stay invested for the longer term. He then concentrated in long term equity investments following the value investment methodology. He is known for identifying a strong trend long before others. He was one of the biggest investors in HDFC Bank post its listing and was seen accumulating it despite stretched valuations and relatively cheaper options available. He has the knack to discern between an outperformer and market performer among equities and is known for his investments in stocks like HDFC Bank, Gillette, VST Ind.s, Crisil etc. He has a penchant for listed MNCs operating in India due to their transparency and professionalism along with a growing product basket. RK Damani's investment philosophy involves buying extremely cheap stocks, which have a huge potential and have witnessed a low demand in the markets; and holding on to them for a very long period.

Mr. Damani operates two investment companies - Bright Star Investments and Derive Investments. He is the promoter/ owner of Avenue Super Markets, the company that controls around more than 120 D-Mart retail store chains in India. He has implemented the value investment style in his business which involves owning the land (bought at relatively cheap prices), keeping the variable cost minimal. Despite being profitable, he did not rush into opening new stores (as normally seen in the industry) but took a slow but convincing growth path to reach its current level, thus creating wealth not only for himself but for his fellow investors too. He enormously values people around him, be it his business partners, employees or family members. Having tasted the fruits of equity culture in markets, he has implemented it in his business by partnering with his employees and awarding them ESOPs, thus making him a 'Niruddha' investor.

Nemish Shah

Nemish Shah is the founder of ENAM Holdings, one of the reputed investment houses in India. ENAM had merged its banking and broking operations with Axis Bank in 2010.

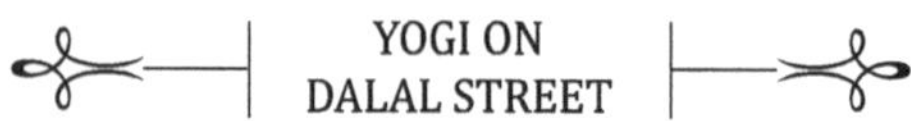

His investment philosophy involves following a fundamental bottom-up approach to investing with a long term investment horizon. He tries to identify structurally well positioned businesses of high quality, which have sustainable competitive advantages along with a reasonably wide moat necessary for long term growth. He places great emphasis on the importance of the management, their integrity and commitment to the business, along with transparency and ethics, while making equity investments. He finds comfort in a management which is single mindedly focused on its business, understands the business like the back of its hand and harbours a vision to make it big. His approach includes identifying the size of the opportunity, company's position and competitive advantage among its peers, management's vision and execution capabilities. He prefers a management which understands capital allocation and applies it in its business. Being a value investor, he then looks for the correct entry price to take a substantially good stake and remains a committed investor to ride the growth phase of the business which generally involves years together. If needed, he hand holds the management in its thick and thin without intervening in the day to day business activities, thus making him an epitome of a Niruddha investor.

Conclusion

Investment is an art and lessons such as those mentioned above are indispensable if one wants to become a great investor. Ergo, out of these five states of mind, the last two stages are most desirable. One should avoid being in the first three states of mind i.e. Kshipta, Mudha and Vikshipta for a prolonged period and once one knows one's position, try to move up the ladder. Ekagra and Niruddha states are the ultimate states of mind that an investor should aim for. Identification of one's state of mind and applying it in one's investing habits helps one create wealth in the long run.

End Note

Hopefully, this book has helped you gain a different perspective on how the mind operates and ways in which you can strengthen your investing behaviour, using our ancient scriptures, especially the Yoga Sutra. Rising up the ladder is the very purpose of our existence and Purusartha clearly states that one should rise in Dharma (right conduct), Artha (prosperity), Kama (object of desire) and Moksha (liberation). Therefore, one should not be apologetic about money, but should rather strive to create wealth and prosperity. In order to create wealth, one must first identify the best asset class that can grow wealth relatively faster than others. Equity emerges a clear winner historically by providing the best returns in the long term world-wide. Hence, one should not ignore equity in the path to wealth creation. Having said that, there is low participation in equity and even within those people who participate, few create wealth. This is because more than market movements, 'investor psychology' plays the most important role in selecting the right stocks at the right time thereby creating wealth. When it comes to psychology or 'the mind', as a subject, there is no better book than the Yoga Sutra, an age old treasure written almost 2500 years back but still very relevant to the modern day world. From this ancient wisdom of Yoga Sutra, I have selected 22 traits in this book. The ones that are positive need to be strengthened and the ones that are negative need to be minimized or stilled.

Now, let's take a quick re-look at what we have learnt so far.

In the first module, we covered the 'Panchaleshas' or the five causes of human suffering namely Avidya (ignorance), Asmita (ego), Raga (attachment), Dvesha (aversion) and Abhinivesha (fear of loss). Avidya is the mother of all Kleshas and from it stems all other kleshas. These Kleshas form the impediments on the road to riches for an investor. They are difficult to eliminate but need to be minimized for one to be a Yogic Investor. If investors are successful in minimizing these five kleshas, they have nearly won half the battle as these 'demons' happen to be the very reasons for major failures in one's investing life.

In the second module, we dwelled on 'Bhavas' which talks about the attitude towards investing. There are 4 bhavas - Dharma (duty), Gyana (knowledge), Vairagya (detachment) and finally Aishwarya (bliss). The bhavas clearly guide us about the right path to be undertaken for a successful investor. One must therefore do the dharma or duty towards planning the future for oneself, one's family, one's work and finally the society at large. Having laid down the path, one must light it to illuminate one's goal with Gyana. Once one has undertaken the path of Dharma and Gyana, they must strive to be in the state of Vairagya which teaches one to be patient, ultimately guiding them towards Aishwarya where one relishes the fruits of investing.

The third module, 'Gunas' is about the defining qualities of an investor. There are 3 gunas - Tamas (inactivity), Rajas (energy) and Sattva (Harmony). One of three gunas dominates us at any particular point in time. A Tamas pradhan investor is lethargic and indifferent about creating wealth while a Rajas pradhan investor is one with a lot of energy to make money which leads to reckless investing. Sattva is a state of harmony between Rajas and Tamas, combining the energy of Rajas with the stability of

Tamas. Sattva is the most desired guna and most conducive state to create wealth.

The fourth module deals with 'Vrittis' which are the variations/fluctuations in the mind, which need to be stilled. The 5 vrittis are Pramana (right knowledge), Viparyaya (wrong knowledge), Vikalpa (imagination), Nidra (sleep) and Smriti (memory). Vrittis can be of two kinds namely klishta and aklishta. Klishta vrittis cause harm while Aklishta vrittis are beneficial to an investor. An investor has to replace klishta vritti using aklishta and endeavour to go beyond it.

Finally, the fifth module speaks about States of 'Chitta' or 5 states of mind - Kshipta (disturbed), Mudha (dull), Vikshipta (occasionally steady), Ekagra (one-pointed) and Niruddha (arrested mind). Both Kshipta & Mudha are undesirable states of mind and are relatively gross in nature, the former being recklessly active while the latter being excessively lethargic. An individual in both these states must uplift himself to a higher state of Ekagra albeit through the Vikshipta route where the mind is mostly distracted but intermittently focused. Having reached Vikshipta, the investor has to elevate to Ekagra state and then finally to be at that state long enough to attain Niruddha, the pinnacle in the investing world.

Just like Yoga, investing is also a broad and complex subject matter and this book covers some of the key financial concepts. I therefore urge everyone to go beyond the concepts explained in this book and explore more about investing to gain mastery in it. To become a good investor, one must practice investment with profound knowledge, devotion and discipline like sadhana.

It is believed that both the goddesses Lakshmi and Saraswati have the power to bestow prosperity upon whomever they choose. The wealth that comes only with Lakshmi's blessings, leaves faster than it arrives. However, those who gain prosperity with the blessings of Saraswati, the goddess of knowledge, never lose their wealth. This is because the source of their prosperity is wisdom gained with self-effort either through the dispassionate self-study or the awakening of intuition through Yoga.

May you become the "Yogic Investor"

Arun Thukral